LANDSCAPE AUSTRALIA

*Cascading rainwater and wind-blown sand have rounded and scored
the surface of Ayres Rock in Uluru National Park.*

LANDSCAPE AUSTRALIA

Images of a colourful land

PUBLISHED BY PTN AUSTRALIA

Pier 35, Suite 9, 263 Lorimer Street, Port Melbourne, Victoria 3207, Australia

Telephone: +613 9681 9166   Email: email@ptn.com.au

Original text by Geoff Gaylard
Revised by Caroline Taylor

Front Cover:
Fracture planes, scree and weathered surfaces catch the sun's last rays, casting dark shadows upon a rock outcrop in Rainbow Valley in central Australia.

Back Cover:
Lone Mangrove tree with roots exposed by the low tide on pristine, South Cowie Beach in Cape Tribulation National Park, far north Queensland, a World Heritage Area.

First published in 1989.

First reprint 1993.

Second reprint 2005.

Published by PTN Australia

ISBN 1 920873 29 5

Printed in China.

PROJECT STAFF

Photographer: PETER WALTON

Text and Original Poetry: GEOFF GAYLARD

Editorial Assistance: ANOUSHKA IBBETSON

Art Direction: JONATHAN BROWNE, BILL HEMMINGS

Peter Walton is a Melbourne based photographer specialising in Australian landscapes. Most of the images in this book are held by his image library Australian Scenics (www.australianscenics.com). The library can be contacted by telephone on 03 9848 9932 or by email at images@australianscenics.com. For further information about Peter Walton's images see inside the back cover of this book.

CONTENTS

◆ ◆

DEDICATION

Dedicated to my wife and co-photographer Margaret. Without her constant encouragement and assistance, this book would not have been possible.

– Peter Walton

LANDSCAPE AUSTRALIA
IMAGES OF A TIMELESS LAND

Australia's extraordinary landscapes are superbly captured in this new edition of *Landscape Australia – Images of a Timeless Land*.

The scenic images reproduced in this publication are a reminder of how lucky we are to live in this unique country. This new edition will, I am sure, inspire more Australians to explore their own land and encourage international visitors to experience its natural attractions and terrific lifestyle.

Australia's landscapes are as diverse as those who live here. Our country offers breathtaking mountain scenery, stunning rainforests, rugged coastlines, sweeping sandy beaches and deserts which come alive after rain.

This publication affords us a wonderful opportunity to appreciate the timeless beauty our country has to offer. I encourage you to reflect on these wonderful images.

John Howard

(John Howard)

This book is a portrait of a unique and fascinating environment. Vast in its magnitude, spectacular in its natural beauty, often forbiddingly wild and desolate, amazingly diverse and richly endowed. Australia is a land of many surprising contrasts. Its abundance of ancient rocks, its generally low and eroded landforms and its remarkably different flora and fauna distinguish this as the oldest of continents; yet in terms of discovery and settlement it is, except for Antarctica, the youngest. Ranked among the richest and most developed of nations, it is predominantly a sparsely settled, arid and isolated place. Bustling, brash and vigorous in its cities, it has an aura of awesome antiquity in its enormous desert interior and endless plains.

Any portrayal must be set within basic parameters. These, even in an overview, permit comparisons to assist understanding and focus attention. In the broadest sense we are focusing on an areas between latitudes 10°41'S and 43°39'S, spanning longitudes 113°09'E to 153°39'E, the extremities of the Australian mainland and its attendant island state, Tasmania.

Seas break vigorously on rocks at Cape Conran in Victoria, forming tidal pools amid littoral shelves.

These, girded by the Indian, Southern and Pacific oceans with the Timor, Arafura and Coral seas to the north, encompass a land area of 7,692,024 square kilometres. This ranks Australia as the sixth largest country on the globe (excluding Antarctica), spanning both tropical and temperate zones. Immediately, another contrast is evident, for in all this huge area there are just over twenty million people.

A free, democratic country of predominantly European descent, with an active policy of multiculturalism and a modern industrialised economy, contemporary Australia is a recognised and active member of the community of nations.

Obviously, another parameter – time – must be considered in order to fully grasp and truly understand the reality of Australia today. It was time, and a very great deal of it, combined with geographical isolation, that produced a period of 'evolutionary quarantine', enabling the markedly different character of Australia to emerge. The slow processes of evolution, unhindered by cross-linking of genetic and other environmental factors from adjacent continents, followed different paths to those found elsewhere and gave Australia its unique flora and fauna.

Time also contributed to Australia's isolation. While warring tribes and conquering armies ceaselessly crossed other continents, Australia remained undisturbed. Very many centuries passed before man developed sufficiently advanced and reliable ships to cross the oceanic barriers concealing and defending the southern continent's shores.

It is not possible to give a precise date to Australia's discovery or unequivocally state any specific event leading mankind to her shores. What *is* certain from archaeological evidence is that Australia has known human habitation for at least 50-70,000 years. The firstcomers were those people now known as Australian Aborigines, who are thought to have come from Asia by way of an ancient land bridge which as since degenerated into the island chain to Australia's north-west. Doubtless, over the millennia, they too evolved differently from their forebears – indeed, many anthropologists classify the 'Australoid' as a distinct racial type.

Waves batter rugged cliffs, at Cape Bridgewater near Portland on Victoria's western coastline.

There is also ample evidence that Malay seamen visited Australia's northern coastline in more recent times, fishing for trepang and shellfish, camping ashore and trading with the Aborigines. Visits by others are suspected but unsubstantiated, and speculations abound. Various historians have postulated theories that Chinese and Arabian navigators knew the northern coastal waters or that Portuguese and Spanish mariners touched upon the eastern seaboard prior to Cook's famous 1770 voyage in the *Endeavour*. If so, no tangible traces of their presence remain which are sufficiently strong to be conclusive proof.

Clearly, it is a fatuous paradox to claim 'discovery' of an already inhabited area! In the context of the various 'discovery' voyages made to Australia we must redefine the word to mean those first sightings or explorations placed as fact on enduring records. The storing of navigational data in durable form was essentially a European achievement, so while recognising that other seafaring races may have valid claims to earlier visits, only the recorded European events will be considered here.

How was it that such a vast land mass lay hidden from the rest of the world for so many centuries? Certainly the *idea* of a southern continent dates from very early times. By the 3rd century BC, Greek sages had disproved the notion of a flat earth and proven it was round. Roughly five hundred years later the noted Greek-Egyptian astronomer and geographer Claudius Ptolemy, advanced the theory that a vast southern continent existed in the southern hemisphere, somewhere to the east of Africa. This was considered as being necessary to balance the earth's globe and prevent it from toppling over!

More than a thousand years were to pass before Ptolemy's theory was given substance.

Huge rugged limestone cliffs breast the surge of the Southern Ocean near Eucla on the Great Australian Bight.

In the latter part of this long period two vital prerequisites to transoceanic travel were developed – a sufficiently strong motivation to risk life and fortune, and a reliable means of long voyaging. The motivation was trade. Since the return of the Venetian explorer Marco Polo from his epic journeying through Asia, a great trade in tea, spices and other commodities was gradually built between Europe and the Orient. So lucrative was this trade that all major nations became deeply involved, often controlling pricing and supply through enormous and powerful commercial empires such as the East India Company.

Maritime trade followed the 1498 route of the Portuguese mariner Vasco da Gama, rounding the Cape of Good Hope and following the eastern seaboard of Africa northwards to Sri Lanka, India and beyond. Strong and sound vessels became necessary both to tackle very rough seas and to accommodate large and valuable cargoes. Slowly, vessels capable of long periods of transoceanic voyaging were evolved.

It was the Dutch, engaged in trade through their major outposts at Batavia (now Jakarta) and Malacca and ranging throughout this region close to Australia's north, who first landed on Australian soil. Our first certain knowledge of such an event dates from 1606 when Willem Janszoon in the *Duyfken* touched ashore on the western coast of the Gulf of Carpentaria. He did not realise the significance of this landfall.

It was also the Dutch who began to seek shorter and swifter routes to their trading centres in the East Indies. Profit was the major motivation but another imperative was avoiding the Portuguese naval strongholds then established in Goa and Sri Lanka.

Waves lap sandy beaches near Waddy Point on Fraser Island.

In 1611 Hendrik Brouwer ran before the prevailing westerly winds east from the Cape of Good Hope for 3,000 miles before steering north to reach Java. Two years later the Dutch East India Company ordered all its vessels to steer this course.

This new route placed ships squarely within the influences of two of the world's great latitudinal windbelts – the Westerlies which sweep across the Southern Ocean, and the South-East Trades which blow northward across the Pacific Ocean from about latitude 30°S, towards the Equator. As the Westerlies shift slightly northwards in the southern winter, the southernmost coasts of Australia fall within their range. Thus the new Dutch navigation orders made it inevitable that sooner or later some ship, underestimating its eastward passage or driven far eastward by gales, would, in turning to the north, encounter the Australian coast.

Basically, this is what occurred with several ships between 1616 and 1622. So it may be said that the European discovery of Australia resulted from its position relative to the westerly windbelt.

The first event happening as described above, was in 1616 when Dirk Hartog in the *Eendracht* landed on an island in Shark Bay. A succession of sightings and landings on the western seaboard followed: in 1618 Lenaert Jacobszoon and Willem Janszoon in the *Mauritius*, in 1619 Frederik de Houtman commanding the *Dordrecht* and the *Amsterdam*, in 1622 the *Leeuwin*, and in 1627 Francois Thijssen sailed the *Golden Zeepaert* along the southern coastline as far as Streaky Bay.

A low swell bursts over a rocky shelf at Thouin Bay on Tasmania's Freycinet Peninusula. Rapid run-off clearly illustrates the sea's erosive power which formed these littoral shelves.

With several vessels now reporting a hitherto unknown coastline the Dutch East India Company began to scent further potential profits. In August 1642, the Dutch Governor-General of the East Indies, Antony van Diemen, ordered Abel Janszoon Tasman to take the *Heemskerk* and *Zeehan* to explore south of the known land mass. Departing from Mauritius, he ran before the westerly winds until he encountered a particularly rugged coast (south-west Tasmania). On 24 November he formally annexed this land for Holland, naming it Antony Van Diemensland. On a subsequent voyage, Tasman left Java in an attempt to penetrate Torres Strait and reach the Pacific Ocean. Failing in this, he charted the coastline from the Gulf of Carpentaria south-west almost to Dirk Hartog Island.

It should be noted that almost all the coastline of two-thirds of the continent had now been visited by the Dutch. However, so much of it was dry and barren that the Dutch East India Company saw little point in further pursuing exploration, and in late 1644 Governor van Diemen and the Council of the Dutch East India Company formally abandoned the search for riches in the still mysterious southern continent. From that point on the Dutch made no significant Australian landfalls.

A huge and aged eucalypt stands tall amid beeches in Pine Valley, within the Cradle Mountain-Lake St Clair National Park. This section of Tasmanian beech forest is listed as a World Heritage area.

Far Right:
Bakers Oven Rock at Port Campbell National Park.

For over a century (1644-1768) relatively little exploration occurred, and attention must turn from the Dutch to the British. Prior to 1770 only two Englishmen sighted Australia. In 1622 the *Tryal* under the command of Captain John Brooke was wrecked on a reef off the Monte Bello Islands with the loss of 97 lives. The 46 survivors reached the safety of Batavia in a ship's boat and pinnace. William Dampier, an English privateer, anchored his *Cygnet* below Cape L'Eveque on the north-west coast of 1688. On his return to England he published a book of his adventures, speculating that although his own observations were of a harsh and unpromising coastline, such an enormous area could well harbour "fruitful lands".

Dampier's book attracted the attention of the British Admiralty which agreed to sponsor him on another voyage. Setting out in the *Roebuck* in 1699, he attempted to round Cape Horn to approach from the east. Frustrated and defeated by adverse winds and rough seas, he went about, and following the course of the Dutch navigators reached the Western Australian coast. This he charted from south of Shark Bay to the Buccaneer Archipelago. Surviving the wrecking of the *Roebuck* in the South Atlantic, he returned to England and again published an account of his travels. This second book aroused interest anew, but failed to prompt further exploration.

St Columba Falls near Pyengana in north-eastern Tasmania show the vigour of a young river. Treeferns proliferate in such moist locations.

The next significant figure was also a writer. Alexander Dalrymple, a former hydrographer for the East India Company, took up a position within the British Admiralty. Possessed by a passionate interest in anything pertaining to the Pacific area, he studied everything available. Among documents he had access to were Dutch material captured in Manila in 1762 during the 'mercantile cold war' being fought throughout the East Indies by the major European powers. These documents hinted at the existence of a strait between New Guinea and the Great South Land. Fired by enthusiasm, Dalrymple expounded his belief in the existence of a vast southern continent, and vigorously urged its settlement in order to expand Britain's maritime power. Published in 1765, this book was given serious consideration by the British Admiralty.

In 1766-67 the Admiralty formulated plans for a scientific voyage to Tahiti to observe the transit of the planet Venus across the disc of the sun. Dalrymple hoped to command this expedition but was passed over in favour of a junior naval officer, Lieutenant James Cook. A former Whitby collier, the *Earl of Pembroke* was obtained, converted and rigged as a barque, renamed the *Endeavour*, and provided for the purposes of the voyage.

On August 26, 1768, the *Endeavour* set sail from Plymouth. Aboard her was Joseph Banks, a botanist and a member of the Royal Society – England's premier scientific establishment – who carried a copy of Dalrymple's book. Also aboard were Dr David Solander, a naturalist, and astronomer Charles Green, together with four artists. These comprised the scientific party, who in addition to observing the transit of Venus, were to study, collect and record specimens of natural history and other items of scientific interest.

Lieutenant Cook also carried papers, among them secret sealed orders not to be opened until the astronomical observations from Tahiti were completed. These proved to be scientific instructions to search for the enormous southern continent Dalrymple had described and was convinced existed.

Sky hues are mirrored in the sand-choked mouth of a stream entering Maingon Bay in south-east Tasmania.

TO

Lieut. Cook Commanding

His Maj^s Bark. Endeavour

By the Commiss^n for executing

the Office of Lord High

Admiral of Gt. Britain &c.

Secret

Whereas we have, in Obedience to the Kings Commands, caused His Maj^s Bark the Endeavour, whereof you are Commander, to be fitted out in a proper manner for receiving such Persons as the Royal Society should think fit to appoint to observe the Passage of the Planet Venus over the Disk of the Sun on the 3^d of June 1769, and for conveying them to such Place to the Southward of the Equinoctial Line as should be judged proper for observ^g that Phenomenon;…so soon as the Observation of the Transit of the Planet Venus shall be finished…you are to proceed to the Southward in order to make discovery of the Continent above mentioned until you arrive in the Lat^{de} of 40°, unless you sooner fall in with it. But not having discover'd it or any distant sign of it in that Run you are to proceed in search of it to the Westw^d between the Lat^{de} beforementioned and the Lat^{de} of 35° until you discover it.

Cook's instructions 1768, quoted C. M. H. Clark

Weather-etched limestone formations in Ben Boyd National Park on the south-east coast.

By June 3, 1769, the astronomical observations being complete, Cook felt free to open his sealed orders which instructed him to sail south as far as latitude 40°S and then turn westward. Reluctantly leaving the warmth of the tropics and hospitality of the Tahitians, the *Endeavour* maintained a southerly course for several weeks until on October 7, the north island of New Zealand hove into view.

Cook and his company spent the next six months meticulously charting the coastlines of the New Zealand islands, proving conclusively that the land they had found was not a part of the great southern continent. It was already evident that Dalrymple's notion of the size of the southern land was grossly exaggerated. Rather dispirited, the company of the *Endeavour* left New Zealand on March 31, sailing under Cook's instructions further to the west.

Early on the morning of April 20, 1770, land was sighted by an officer, Lieutenant Zachary Hicks. This proved to be the south-eastern tip of the long-sought southern continent, and today bears the name Cape Hicks. The date of sighting is listed in Cook's log as April 19 – he failed to make allowance for gaining a day in crossing what is now what is now known as the International Date Line!

Steering northward, Cook now commenced a tour of discovery along Australia's eastern seaboard remarkable not only for the feats of seamanship and painstaking survey it involved, but also for its constant stream of startling environmental, botanical, zoological and anthropological revelations. For here was a diverse coastline over 3,000 kilometres long, offering sheltered harbours, lush and fertile plains, forested ranges and the largest, most complex and teeming coral structure in the world.

Reflected hoodoo at Barn Hill
near Broome.

Progressively surveying and charting, collecting specimens and recording diverse scientific data, the *Endeavour* probed slowly northward. Surviving hull damage, careening and the many dangers of the labyrinthine channels of the Great Barrier Reef, she arrived at the northernly extremity of Cape York. Here, on August 22, Cook ascended the highest point – an offshore island – and surveying the distances, could discern no further land mass. Hoisting the English flag, he took possession on behalf of his king, of the entire eastern coast. He named it New South Wales. The site of this event is now known as Possession Island.

Exceptional seamanship apart, Cook's achievement on this voyage was twofold: he alerted Europe to the suitability of the land for settlement, and by precisely establishing the location of the eastern coast, proved that the Great South Land was not nearly as vast as many had assumed it to be. This voyage had an influence, among several factors, on the British government's decision to establish a settlement at Botany Bay.

Much maritime exploration remained to be done. Those few coastal maps which existed were compiled in piecemeal fashion from various sources spanning over a century. However, the generalised outline of the mainland was close to complete, and as Matthew Flinders put it, "The direction given to some parts of the coast, approaches too near the truth, for the whole to have been marked from conjecture alone."

Both French and English navigators played a role in filling in the unknown gaps and accurately surveying the stretches of coastline previously sighted. Most significant of the French explorers were d'Entrecasteaux and Baudin. Bruni d'Entrecasteaux, commanding the *Recherche* and *Esperance*, charted the southern shoreline of Western Australia in 1792. Sailing further south-east he encountered and surveyed southern Tasmania, discovering the Riviere du Nord (now the Derwent River).

A further French expedition of 1801-03 under the command of Nicolas Baudin, and utilising the well-equipped research vessels *Le Geographe* and *Le Naturaliste*, charted the southern coast from Discovery Bay to Cape Adieu. The expedition met with Matthew Flinders' sloop the *Investigator* in a bay near Kangaroo Island, an event which Flinders commemorated by naming the site Encounter Bay. The Baudin expedition excited speculation that the French intended colonising Tasmania.

Alluvial flats border the Cambridge Gulf, cut by the Ord and Durack Rivers, near Wyndham, on Australia's north-west coast.

To the British goes overall credit for mapping the entire seaboard in thorough fashion. Several individuals contributed, but undoubtedly the most notable were firm friends George Bass and Matthew Flinders, and later, Lieutenant Phillip King. It is a tribute to the extraordinary skills and seamanship of these men that some of their charts were still used as reliable navigation aids until the last century.

Bass, a surgeon, and Flinders, then a midshipman, arrived in Sydney aboard HMS *Reliance* on September 25, 1795. Bass brought with him a diminutive 2.5 metre boat named *Tom Thumb*. The two young men shared a passion for exploration, and soon began a series of exploratory coastal voyages in the tiny craft. In April of 1796 they made a detailed examination of Port Hacking and later explored the Illawarra coast.

On December 3, 1797, Bass, unaccompanied by Flinders, journeyed by whaleboat further southwards along the eastern shoreline. Rounding Wilsons Promontory, the southern extremity of the mainland, he discovered and entered Western Port, a major bay. On this trip he wrote of his suspicion that a strait existed between the mainland and Tasmania.

The Pinnacles on Fraser Island, a large sand island off the eastern coast, mimic mountain ranges.

Upon his return to Sydney, the sloop *Norfolk* was specially fitted out to investigate the suspected strait. Together, Bass and Flinders sailed south in her on October 7, 1798. Skirting the northern Tasmanian coast, they steered south along the rugged west coast and completed a circumnavigation of Tasmania, thus proving it be an island. This voyage, by proving the existence of the strait now bearing Bass's name, opened an important new route to Sydney. It also prompted theories that other little-known bays and gulfs could possibly be the openings of straits between islands, and that Australia was possibly an archipelago.

Departing from Sydney in July the following year, Flinders, without Bass, explored the northern coast of New South Wales. He then took ship back to England. Promoted for his exploits, he was given command of the 334-ton *Investigator* and ordered to make a complete examination of the Australian coastline. He sailed from England on July 18, 1801, to begin a voyage which would stamp him as one of the world's greatest cartographers.

The *Investigator* arrived at Cape Leeuwin, Western Australia on December 6, 1801, to begin her mammoth task. In the succeeding months a detailed study was made of the southern coast, including a trip up Spencer Gulf to test a theory that the Southern Ocean might connect with the Arafura Sea. In April 1802, on the completion of this particular detour, the *Investigator* sighted and contacted Baudin's French expedition in Encounter Bay. By June/July she had reached Sydney.

Reprovisioned, she departed on July 22, sailing along the north-east coast. Flinders discovered the harbour at Bowen and a passage – now known as Flinders Passage – through Torres Strait. Surveying as she went, the *Investigator* followed the shoreline to return to Sydney on June 9, 1803. Flinders had become the first circumnavigator of Australia and had established beyond doubt that the continent was one land mass and not a series of islands.

Gentle waves roll ashore in Sugarloaf Bay within the Myall Lakes National Park, adjacent to Port Stephens on the eastern coast.

Investigator was now unseaworthy and Flinders took ship back to England to present his charts to the Admiralty. He left aboard the *Porpoise* which ran onto Wreck Reef off the eastern seaboard. Sailing back to Sydney in a makeshift cutter, Flinders took command of the schooner *Cumberland*, returned to rescue the marooned *Porpoise* crew, and resumed his journey to England.

His ill-fortune was not over: his ship leaking dangerously, he put into port at the French-possessed island of Mauritius. Here he was taken prisoner as England was again at war with France. Released eight years later, he made his way to London to publish his charts. To his chagrin, he found that Freycinet and Peron, geographers of Baudin's expedition, had already published accounts of their Australian journey, naming every major feature. Flinders' book *A Voyage to Terra Australis* which advocated the name Australia for the new continent, was published in London on July 18, 1814. Matthew Flinders never saw the book, as he died the following day.

As comprehensive as Flinders' work had been, the sheer enormity and complexity of Australia's coasts required further surveys to be done to provide detailed clarification. Lieutenant Phillip King took up this challenge. In 1819,

Acacia, Chorizema and Hardenbergia all bloom among the bracken bordering Lefroy Brook at the Cascades, near Pemberton, Western Australia.

Far Right:
Jagged orange sandstone juts from the end of Eighty Mile Beach at Cape Keraudren in Western Australia's north.

in the *Mermaid*, he charted Macquarie Harbour in Tasmania. Later the same year he further explored the convoluted coastline of northern Australia. As commander of the brig *Bathurst* he surveyed parts of Western Australia, including Rottnest Island, in 1821. Other voyages were undertaken and by late 1822 his task was completed.

The skills, courage and perseverance of these men should not be undervalued. The Australian coastline is a particularly forbidding one for the greater part of its length. These mariners faced the constant dangers of the unknown for long periods and often in barely adequate craft, entirely bereft of aid or rescue

should disaster strike. Their achievements are a triumph of the human spirit over the unforgiving seas.

In August 1786 the British government decided to found a penal colony in New South Wales, thus initiating the European settlement of Australia. Historians make various claims about their motives for doing so. Some believe it was to provide a new destination for convict transportation, as the traditional outlets were denied to Britain by the American revolt. Others see it as an expansion of geopolitical influence or the acquisition of a trading base closer to the East Indies spice trade. Still others believe that Australia was perceived as having the potential to be a valuable source of flax and tall timber. Influenced by Joseph Banks' glowing reports and Cook's reference to "fine meadows", Botany Bay was chosen as the site for the settlement.

In May 1787, the eleven small vessels comprising the First Fleet mustered off Portsmouth. They were a sorry lot. The flagship, HMS *Sirius* of 600 tons, had been burnt to the waterline in the shipyards, cheaply rebuilt and used as a victualler in the East Indies. Hastily overhauled, fitted with 20 guns and renamed, she was given to Phillip as a warship for the Fleet's protection – and was the best and largest of them all!

Low eucalypts loom through the mist in an alpine area of the Wonnangatta-Moroka National Park.

Far Right:
Sedimentary rocks display severe weathering effects in the glow of sunset at Gantheaume Point, near Broome on the north-western coast.

The other naval ship, HMS *Supply* of only 170 tons was described in Lieutenant Phillip King's journal as "much too small for a long voyage … not being able to carry any quantity of provisions … sailing very ill renders her a very improper vessel for this service". The transports *Alexander*, *Scarborough*, *Friendship*, *Prince of Wales*, *Charlotte* and *Lady Penrhyn* were renowned as especially heavy sailers. The total tonnage of the Fleet, including the store ships was 3,072 tons burthen. Shipboard conditions were appalling, and they carried over a thousand people – three-quarters of them convicted felons.

On May 13, they set sail under Captain Arthur Phillip, a retired naval officer of German extraction. A voyage of some sixteen thousand miles via South

America, the Cape of Good Hope in South Africa, the Antarctic Circle, then
east to Tasmania and north to Botany Bay lay ahead of them.

After a troubled eight month voyage with many deaths en route, (36 men and
4 women), they attained their target. HMS *Supply*, with Phillip aboard, sailed
into Botany Bay on January 18, 1788. Those aboard anticipating an earthly
paradise ripe for colonisation were bitterly disappointed.

Botany Bay was wide open to the sea, affording little protection for the ships.
The water supply, ample for Cook's one ship *Endeavour*, was totally inadequate
for the Fleet's eleven vessels or for a permanent settlement. Sand dunes,
swamps, scrub and infertile low-lying land stamped it as clearly unsuitable
for colonisation. Within two days the remainder of the Fleet reached the
rendezvous and Phillip hastily decided to move to a small cove in the deepwater
harbour of Port Jackson, a protected bay some miles to the north.

The chosen site, Sydney Cove, was far more suitable offering shelter, good
water and timber. Here, at a formal parade of ships' companies and marines
the proclamation of the colony was made on February 7, 1788.

*Jagged pinnacles pierce the clouds
near Federation Peak in Tasmania's
South West National Park.*

Also, formal possession of the land, on behalf of the British Crown, was taken with the public reading of Captain Phillip's commission issued to him on October 12, 1786 and amplified on April 2, 1787. The commission appointed him

> Captain-General and Governor-in-Chief in and over our territory called New South Wales, extending from the Northern Cape or extremity of the coast called Cape York, in the latitude of ten degrees thirty-seven minutes south, to the southern extremity of the said territory of New South Wales or South Cape, in the latitude of forty-three degrees thirty-nine minutes south and of all the country inland, westward as far as the one hundred and thirty-fifth degree of east longitude, reckoning from the meridian of Greenwich, including all the islands adjacent in the Pacific Ocean within the latitude aforesaid of ten degrees thirty-seven minutes south and forty-three degrees thirty-nine minutes south.

These words encompass an enormous territory. To govern it, Phillip was given wide powers, both civil and military. He could appoint justices of the peace, coroners, constables and other necessary officers, pass judgement on criminals, exact fines, order arrests, pardon, reprieve, remit sentences, levy armed forces "for the resisting and withstanding of all enemies and rebels both at sea and on

An accumulation beach is washed by surf near Quondolo Point at the Ben Boyd National Park in southern New South Wales.

land", execute martial law, erect fortifications, exercise naval powers, control finances, grant lands – in short, he had absolute powers limited only by his ability, conscience and circumstances. Of course, with this absolute power went absolute accountability, and he was ultimately responsible for all the minutiae of the colony's existence.

The British government chose their man well for this extraordinary appointment. His naval record of service was good but not distinguished. A somewhat delicate and apparently nervous man in manner, his exterior hid a character of great determination, incorruptible honesty and imaginative vision. Both intelligent and sensitive, he was capable of decisive action. This was fortunate, for in its founding years the fate of the settlement was often to depend on strong leadership.

An urgent goal of colonial settlement is rapid self-sufficiency. For Sydney, lines of supply from England were so tenuous and time costly as to be useless. This had been foreseen by Lord Sydney, a prime mover in the scheme to establish an Australian penal colony. In his 'Heads of Plan' document submitted to the British government, he included lists of equipment he considered fundamental to attaining self-sufficiency in the first years.

Necessary Implements:

Iron in bars	Soap
Forges and anvils	Hatts and caps
Spades and shovels	Wheels of barrows
Mattocks	Seeds and plants
Spikes and nails	Articles of trade with natives of the
Pitchforks	island, &c.
Axes of sorts	Window glass
Iron crows and wedges	Grain of sorts
Saws of sorts	Fishing tackle
Large hammers	Gardening tools
Mills	Carpenters' do.
Grindstones	Smiths' tools
Cutlery	Shoemakers' do.
Cooking utensils	Bricklayers' do.
Iron pots of sorts	Masons' do.
Shoes and leather	Coals as ballast
Linnen and woollen cloth	Some leaden pumps, &c.
Tinware	Scythes
Thread, needles, &c.	Pewter and earthernware.
Stockings	

List of Tools, Utensils &c., necessary for the Convicts and Marines intended to proceed to New South Wales.

Spades, 1, @ 3s.; shovels, 1, @ 3s.; hoes, 3 for each man, @ 9d; felling axe, 1, @ 3s; hatchet, 1, @ 1s; knife, 1, @ 6d. each; gimblet, wooden bowls, platters, and spoons, 6d. for each man.

A gnarled old Baobab tree supports birds' nests in the Kimberley Ranges of Western Australia.

	£	s.	d.
The articles necessary to each man amounts to 12s. 6d., which for 700 men will be	437	10	0
General Stock			
Crosscut saws, 40, @ 10s. each	20	0	0
Hand saws, 1 for every 4 men, @ 5s. each	43	15	0
Frame saws, 40, @ 16s. each	32	0	0
Adzes, 100, @ 2s. each	10	0	0
Broad axes, 100, @ 2s. 6d. each	12	10	0
Hammers, 1 for every 4 men, @ 1s. each	8	15	0
Augers, 140, @ 1s. each	7	0	0
Drawing knives, 140, at 1s.	7	0	0
Chissles and gouges, 300, @ 7d. each	8	15	0
Planes, 100, @ 2s. 6d. each	12	10	0
Iron forges, anvils, and hammers, 10, @ £3	30	0	0
Grindstones, 30, @ 10s. 6d. each	15	15	0
Wheelbarrows, 40, @ 10s. each	20	0	0
Pickaxes, 50, @ 5s. each	12	10	0
Ploughs, 12, @ £4 each	48	0	0
Iron hand mills, 40, @ £2 each	80	0	0
Cooper's tools, 10 setts, @ £1 15s. each	17	10	0
Carried forward	£823	10	0

Rocky peaks and long sharp ridges are typical of folded formations. These rocky pinnacles jut skywards near Arkaroola, in South Australia's Flinders Ranges.

	£	s.	d.
Brought forward...	823	10	0
Nails of diff't sizes, @ 2s. 9d. p'r 1,000, ab't 10 barrels	100	0	0
Spikes, 2,000, @ £1 10s. p'r 100..	30	0	0
Hinges, 200 pairs, @ 8d. each	6	13	4
Locks, 100, @ 1s. each..	5	0	0
Bar iron, flat and square, 10 ton, @ £17	170	0	0
Glass, 1,000 squares, @ 8d. per doz	33	6	8
Fishing lines, hooks, nets, needles, twine, &c	100	0	0
	£1,268	10	0

Estimate of clothing to serve a male convict for one year.

	£	s.	d.
....			
Jackets, 2, 4s, 6d...	0	9	0
Wollen drawers, 4, @ 2s..	0	8	0
Hat, 1, @ 2s. 6d	0	2	6
Shirts, 3, @ 3s	0	9	0
Worsted stockings, 4 p'r, @ 1s..	0	4	0
Frocks, 3, @ 2s. 3d...	0	6	9
Trousers, 3, @ 2s. 3d...	0	6	9
Shoes, 3, @ 4s. 6d.	0	13	6
	£2	19	6

Isolated coastal stacks, part of the Twelve Apostles group, stand offshore at Victoria's Port Campbell National Park. This rugged coast has many interesting examples of eroded shoreline formations.

Far Right:
Fissured and stained sandstone cliffs reflect in the quiet waters of the Geike Gorge in the Leopold Ranges of north-western Australia.

The expense of clothing female convicts may be computed to amount to the same sum.

A proportion for two years to be provided.

These lists are evidence of the thorough planning of the venture, which despite both unforeseen circumstances and sometimes less than ideal execution, proved vital to the settlement's survival. Many problems did plague the founding of the new settlement, but under the extraordinary circumstances, blame cannot be laid on inadequate long-term planning.

Of all the problems the infant colony faced, the most urgent issue was food supply. Fish were available, but regular catches could not be relied upon. Many of the seeds brought from England had been spoiled in transit and would not

germinate. In any case, few of the colonists had any knowledge of farming, the seasons differed radically from those of the northern hemisphere, and the local soil was hard, dry and barren. Livestock strayed or fell victim to Aborigines or dingoes and it became impractical to rely on them for a sustainable source of fresh meat. Some edible native animals and birds existed but they were too elusive to provide a reliable food resource.

Clearly, the answer to the problem was farming, but the nearby soil was unsuitable. Also, converting rugged wilderness into arable fields was too arduous and time consuming. During the colony's first year only eight acres were cleared. For self-sufficiency to be achieved, easily cleared and fertile land was vital. It was this survival imperative that produced the immediate and ongoing impetus to explore.

Waterborne exploration was the easiest course, and several naval officers, including Governor Phillip, were active in this pursuit. It was Phillip who discovered and named the Hawkesbury River and Pittwater to the north of Port Jackson. Such expeditions were useful, but limited in scope and practicality. However, farming land was found and utilised and gradually the spectre of wholesale starvation was dispelled.

The settlement at Sydney was an essential beachhead for the European colonisation of the continent – but the problem of penetrating the interior remained unsolved. Port Jackson is surrounded by highlands, most notably the Blue Mountains. These presented an impassable barrier severely limiting the landward spread of European settlement.

The Blue Mountains are a portion of the Eastern Highlands, a continuous mountain range which roughly parallels the coastline from the north to the south of the continent. Only two natural and passable gaps through exist. These are the gaps made by the Hunter River and Kilmore Gap, a pass north of Melbourne thought to have been cut by the Murray River in very ancient times. As the rest of this range is extremely rugged and seemingly impenetrable, significant settlement was confined to the area between Sydney and the Hawkesbury River for a quarter of a century. A small coal-based settlement existed at the Hunter River mouth and offshore penal colonies had been established at both Norfolk Island and Tasmania, but major pastoral expansion remained blocked by the Blue Mountains.

Far Right:
At the edge of low forest, two eucalypts frame the Jamison Valley beneath an escarpment of the Blue Mountains.

Between 1802 and 1813, several attempts were made to cross this range, notably by George Caley and also by Ensign Francis Barrallier. These were frustrated by the broken terrain and dense undergrowth. In May of 1813, George Blaxland, William Charles Wentworth and William Lawson made another attempt. Unlike their precursors, they avoided the tangled and misleading valleys and kept to the more openly timbered ridges. They were successful in finding a route across and a passage was opened giving settlers access to the inland plains.

The significance of this event cannot be overestimated. The only comparable colonisation of a continent was the settlement of North America, most of which occurred in the same historical period, utilising a similar level of technology. There, the great river systems provided natural corridors into the interior. From the founding of the first Spanish outposts on the mainland to a point where the broad outlines of the interior were known, took more than three hundred years. The United States region, with an area similar to Australia's took two hundred years to be known in the same way. The basic outlines of the Australian interior were known within three-quarters of a century from Blaxland, Wentworth and Lawson's Blue Mountains passage, and within a century of the First Fleet's arrival.

The Cambridge Gulf, near Wyndham in Australia's north-west, has sinuous shores formed of alluvial flats deposited by the Ord and Durack Rivers.

Far Right:
The Three Sisters group consists of deeply fissured rock stacks abutting the edge of the main escarpment marking the boundary of the Eastern Highlands near Katoomba in New South Wales.

This is especially remarkable considering that the Australian interior is generally a much more inhospitable terrain than that which was encountered in America.

The crossing of the Blue Mountains began a period of expansion and exploration hitherto impossible and different in character to that which had preceded it. Prior to 1813 exploration was usually undertaken on an official or quasi-official basis, mostly by individuals supported by scant resources. From this time onward though, Australia began to arouse a great deal of scientific curiosity overseas, and this, coupled with the pastoral boom brought about by the discovery of the inland plains, led to the well-equipped expedition becoming the norm. Often exploration groups were led either by scientists (such as Cunningham) or surveyors (like Mitchell or Oxley) and included

botanists, geologists or artists in a supportive role. Potential rewards were becoming apparent and the move to expand outward was gathering impetus.

Excited by discoveries of Blaxland, Wentworth and Lawson, George William Evans determined to continue their explorations further. Crossing the ranges by their route, he pushed further inland. In 1813 he discovered and named the Macquarie River and in 1815 he encountered the Lachlan River. Both rivers flowed westward, arousing speculation about a possible inland sea. This riddle of rivers was not to be resolved for another fifteen years.

It was Governor Macquarie's wish to extend exploration of the hinterland, as pastoral land on the Cumberland Plain was becoming scarce. In April 1817, the Surveyor-General, John Oxley, with George Evans as his second in command and botanist Allan Cunningham, mounted an expedition to determine the course of the Lachlan River and generally investigate the interior. This expedition, equipped with both boats and carts, departed from Bathurst on April 19, 1817, reaching the banks of the Lachlan River on April 25. Several miles upstream from the point reached by Evans in 1815, the boats were launched. Observations were made from the boats and by men on horseback riding along the banks as they proceeded downstream.

On May 12, the expedition halted. Ascending a hill to view the surrounding country, Oxley realised that the area from west-north-west to the north was a flooded marshland into which the river flowed. Attempts were made to force a passage onwards but the water became too shallow and weed-choked to continue. Abandoning the boats, they set out south-westwards on horseback.

By June 4, they reached their most southerly position, slightly north of the present site of Griffith. Rocky ground and water shortage prevented further progress, so the party rode to the north. On June 23, they were surprised by the discovery of a strong-flowing stream, again apparently flowing generally westward. Oxley believed it may have been the Lachlan River which they left nearly five weeks earlier. Evans, however, thought it could be the Macquarie River.

Queensland's Glasshouse Mountains, viewed here from Mount Beerburrum, typify the shapes formed when volcanic plugs and intrusions are exposed by erosion. The distinctive foreground plants are grasstrees.

On July 7, leaving the main party encamped, Oxley attempted to follow this stream but was forced to turn back the same day as it was too inaccessible. Here, at the most westerly campsite, details of the expedition were buried in a wine bottle, beneath a marked tree. Years later Major Mitchell sought the tree, but it has never been found.

The return journey began on July 9, and after enduring many difficulties, the expedition regained Bathurst on August 29. They had been away for nineteen weeks and travelled 1,200 miles, recording details of previously unknown country.

Oxley wrote of this journey:

> "… I was forced to come to the conclusion, that the interior of this vast country is a marsh and uninhabitable … I think it a probable conjecture that this river is the channel by which all the waters rising in those ranges of hills to the westward of Port Jackson, known by the name of the Blue Mountains, and which do not fall into the sea on the east coast, are conveyed to these immense inland marshes; its sinuous course causing it to overflow its banks on a much higher level than the present, and in consequence, forming those low wet levels …"

Governor Macquarie was well satisfied with his Surveyor-General's efforts and reports. He appointed Oxley as the leader of another expedition to explore the course of the Macquarie River.

A depot was established in the Wellington Valley, and in early June 1818 the expedition set out. The same procedure of using boats and land teams was adopted, and progress downriver went smoothly. But on June 30, as Oxley was riding on the riverbank, he noticed that the river ahead was breaking its banks and spreading rapidly across the surrounding plains. Alarmed by this flooding and concerned for the safety of the party, he ordered an immediate retreat for safer ground.

An enormous old Beech overshadows moss and ferns in Pine Valley, a World Heritage area in Tasmania's Cradle Mountain-Lake St Clair National Park.

The main party established a camp, and Oxley, conscious of potential hazards, took four volunteers in the larger boat and proceeded cautiously downstream on July 2. He wrote:

> "The knowledge of its [the river's] actual termination, if at all attainable, was, however, a matter of deep importance, and would tend to throw some light on the obscurity in which the interior of this vast country is still involved. My ardent desire to investigate as far as possible this interesting question, determined me to take the large boat, and with four volunteers to proceed down the river as long as it continued navigable."

After about twenty miles of rowing and drifting upon the current, no land was visible. On July 3, Oxley wrote: "I was sanguine in my expectations of soon entering the long sought for Australian sea." To his puzzlement, his progress was blocked shortly thereafter by a seemingly endless maze of tangled reeds. He reported "… but if an opinion may be permitted to be hazarded from actual appearances, mine is decidedly in favour of our being in the immediate vicinity of an inland sea, or lake, most probably a shoal one …" He was then at latitude 30°45'S, an area now known as Macquarie Marshes.

Scattered grasses help to stabilise extensive coastal sand dunes at St Helens Point on Tasmania's east coast.

◆◆◆◆◆◆◆◆◆◆◆◆◆◆◆◆◆◆◆◆◆◆◆◆◆◆◆◆◆

Oxley and his volunteers returned to the main party, camped near Mount Forster at latitude 31°15'S. In the interim, George Evans had probed eastward and reported finding a river and favourable ground for travelling. Oxley decided to continue in that direction. On July 27, they arrived at the river, which Oxley named the Castlereagh.

Following the Castlereagh River brought them to a well-timbered range of volcanic peaks which they named Arbuthnot's Range, but now known by the Aboriginal name Warrumbungles. Another prominent range was visible to the north-east and the expedition made for it, only to be turned back by excessively boggy ground. Retracing his route, Oxley glimpsed and named the distant Liverpool Plains. The range they had approached, now known as the Nandewar Ranges, was bypassed to the south, and on September 2, the Peel River was discovered and named.

The expedition then scaled the Great Dividing Range, experiencing little difficulty until confronted by precipitous cliffs above the upper Apsley River. A brief westerly retreat and south-easterly detour brought them to the headwaters of the Hastings River and within sight of the sea. Descending to the shoreline near the site of Port Macquarie, the party attempted to trace the

The remnants of a 'petrified forest' formation glow in golden light atop a cliff at Cape Bridgewater near Portland in Victoria.

Far Right:
Deserted old stone cottage in canola crop near Burra.

coast southward, but many arduous detours around swamps frustrated this. Finally reaching Port Stephens, the expeditioners sailed to Sydney.

Oxley was convinced of the existence of an inland sea. Reports of both his 1817 and 1818 expeditions were later to influence Governor Darling to support Sturt and Mitchell in mounting another exploration of the inland river system.

In late 1820 Governor Macquarie issued 'Order 25' which officially sanctioned grazing outside the Cumberland Plains. This initiated the movement of settlers inland, aided in 1823 when Archibald Bell, of Richmond, found a shorter and less rugged route across to Bathurst on the northern side of the Grose Valley. Northward and southward expansion was also beginning. A young Australian-born bushman, Hamilton Hume, visited Berrima between 1814 and 1818. In 1819, in the company of James Meehan, he discovered Lake Bathurst. In 1821 a penal settlement was founded at Port Macquarie, and in the same year, Hume, riding with George Barber and W. H. Broughton, discovered the Yass Plains while en route to the Gunning district to establish a pastoral station.

Settlement along the south coast began when Sydney merchants Edward Wollstonecraft and Alexander Berry established an enormous estate in the Shoalhaven River district in 1822. That same year Hume, Berry and Lieutenant Johnstone penetrated the upper reaches of the Clyde River and journeyed close to the present side of Braidwood.

William Hilton Hovell, a former naval commander, had settled near Camden and taken an interest in exploring the surrounding country. He discovered the Burragorang Valley in 1823. Governor Brisbane intended to despatch an expedition in search on an overland route from Lake Bathurst to the Port

Near Wittenoom in the Hamersley Range, Pilbara region.

Far Right:
Ferns and mosses thrive in the Carnarvon Gorge, home to some very ancient plants including a species of palm now extinct everywhere else.

Phillip district – discovered in 1802 by Lieutenant John Murray – and Hume and Hovell were favoured as leaders; but the project was abandoned. Hovell then suggested to Hume that they share the costs of a private expedition, and a party was formed of themselves, six other men, two carts, five bullocks and three horses. The government gave them its blessing, a tent, tarpaulin, some firearms and ammunition.

On October 17, 1824, the expedition left Hume's Gunning district station on a westerly course. They encountered their first obstacle upon reaching the banks of the Murrumbidgee River. Late rains had swollen the river, which was still rising.

Utilising a cart as an improvised ferry, a successful fording was made. By October 26, as they were encountering rougher terrain, the carts, with part of the provisions, were abandoned in the hope of recovery on the homeward journey. Ahead lay southward trending ranges.

By November 3, after sighting some small plains, a river was reached and named the Medway. Today it is known as the Tumut River. The ranges were becoming increasingly difficult, and descending the western side of the present

Water cascades over hard igneous rock at Cephissus Falls, a charming location within Tasmania's beech forests. Cordylines edge the stream's banks.

Bago Range, south of where the township of Tumut now stands, the party nearly lost both a man and a bullock. Five days later, as the party stopped by a stream, the leaders climbed a hill to determine their onward course. A major discovery was made when:

> "… [we] were suddenly surprised by a sight, to the utmost degree magnificent. Mountains, of a conoidal form, and of an apparently immense height, and some of them covered about one fourth of their height with snow, were now seen extending semicircularly from the S.E. to S.S.W. at the supposed distance of about twenty miles."

These great ranges were named the South Australian Alps.

Soon the steep ranges were left behind and the party was travelling on less hilly, thinly timbered ground. Early on November 16, the land fell slowly and the expedition suddenly encountered a large and deep river, which they named the Hume. So difficult were the banks and so girded by lagoons, that detours were made to find a passable ford. On November 21, a crossing was effected and the journey resumed.

Another river, the Ovens, was forded on November 25. Almost twenty miles south they sighted and named Mount Buffalo and veered westward to avoid the high ranges. The terrain remained hilly and cut by numerous watercourses and on December 3 they discovered and named the Goulburn River. December 8 and 9 were spent skirting a hill which they named Mount Disappointment; both leaders had attempted to climb it but were defeated by impenetrable dead timber and thick scrub.

Their hard-won objective, Port Phillip Bay, was attained on December 16, its waters prolific with fish and wildfowl. The expedition travelled down the shoreline to the entrance of Corio Bay, where deceived by the sight of the Bellarine Peninsula projecting into Port Phillip, they made the error of assuming they had reached Western Port and were viewing French Island.

Only two days were spent at their goal, and the return journey commenced on December 18, following the outward route closely but with a northward detour to avoid the arduous country around Mount Disappointment. The homeward journey was difficult; fatigue was evident, yet a shortage of provisions enforced a more rapid pace. On January 4 they again forded the Hume River, and still about 150 miles from the nearest habitation, distributed the last food ration. This had to last until they recovered the abandoned carts and extra stores, left behind the previous October. Hastening ahead of the main party, the leaders found their depot on January 16, twelve days after their last provisions had been apportioned. Of this forced march their journal records: "The cattle were now so crippled…it was necessary to cover their feet with moccasins, made of kangaroo skins…". The men suffered also.

Sunset light on snow at Mount Hotham Alpine National Park.

Reprovisioned from the carts, the expedition had little further difficulty. All arrived safely at Hume's station on January 18, 1824. Both Hume and Hovell received grants of 1,200 acres of land in recognition of their services and achievement.

As Hume and Hovell pioneered the way south, much else was happening to open up the country. Graziers were pushing the frontiers further from Sydney in a thrust to the south-west. The major route was through the Bargo Bush to Sutton Forest, then across Cockbundoon Range to the Goulburn Plains, in a generalised movement greatly extending the scope of settled land.

In Tasmania too, settlement was spreading. In 1804, settlements were established in both north and south, on the Derwent and Tamar rivers. The influx of Norfolk Island deportees in 1807-08 saw holdings established at New Norfolk, Pittwater and Norfolk Plains. The arrival of Tasmania's first free immigrants in 1815 brought further development, particularly in the Midlands districts. By this year of 1823, several settlements were firmly established between Hobart and Launceston.

It was also the year in which Allan Cunningham, a distinguished botanist who had accompanied Oxley, began, as a leader in his own right, a series of overland treks which placed him among the important explorers of Australia. Cunningham made several excursions throughout the region of southern Queensland and northern New South Wales. He discovered the rivers Namoi,

Gwydir, Dumaresq and Condamine, but more importantly, found Pandora's Pass and Cunninghams Gap. These two natural passes gave access to the vast and fertile pastoral lands of the Liverpool Plains and Darling Downs.

The riddle of the rivers remained unsolved, and as a consequence of Oxley's observations and conjecture, the theory of an inland sea was widely accepted. In 1828, drought was widespread, giving rise to an opportunity to investigate the formerly inaccessible regions of the Macquarie River. Captain Charles Sturt, a military man, persuaded Governor Darling to agree to the formation of a government-assisted expedition into the hinterland to discover the course of the Macquarie River.

On December 7, 1828, the expedition departed from the government depot in the Wellington Valley. Sturt was leader with Hamilton Hume as his second in command, and the party consisted of two soldiers and eight prisoners. Utilising boats and horses, they followed Oxley's general route and met several groups of friendly Aborigines on the way to the Macquarie Marshes, whence they arrived on December 26.

Splitting the party, they generally established the boundaries of the marshes without discovering the river's re-emergence. In the process of scouring the surrounding country, the Bogan and Darling rivers were discovered and named, as were Mount Oxley and the D'Urban group of hills which includes Mount Gunderbrooka as its highest peak.

Everlasting daisies thrive at Victoria's Mount Howitt, adding vivid colour to sombre foliage.

Far Right:
An old River Red Gum's arching bough frames a view of Lake Bulla in the Hattah-Kulkyne National Park in Victoria's north-west.

Short of fresh drinking water, Sturt retreated to a previously arranged depot at Mount Harris for replenishment and rest. From here, he struck east-north-east for the Castlereagh River. Finding it dry, he followed the riverbed back to the Darling. Returning to Mount Harris, Sturt decided to cross the marshes in the hope that the falling water levels would provide the group with a relatively easier passage through. This change of route brought them to the junction of the Darling and Castlereagh rivers and thence to the junction of the Castlereagh and Macquarie. Thus it was proven that these rivers were tributaries of the Darling, so fulfilling the objective of the expedition.

Despite hardships suffered on the 1828-29 journey, Sturt applied to the Governor to lead another expedition to trace the course of the Darling River. Governor Darling though, was more interested in the newly-discovered Murrumbidgee River and appointed Sturt leader of an expedition to determine its complete course.

Accordingly Sturt, accompanied by George McLeay and a sizeable party, left Sydney on November 3, 1829, to accomplish this task. By November 27 they arrived at the junction of the Tumut and Murrumbidgee and set off along the banks, following a downstream course into unexplored country. All progressed well until Christmas Day when, approaching the junction of the Lachlan River, the Murrumbidgee became choked with reeds. Sturt dreaded a similar situation to that of the Macquarie Marshes and made camp.

The next day, scouting ahead with McLeay, he became convinced that the reeds could be successfully negotiated and that the river would hold good for several miles. Back at camp, he ordered a hut and wharf constructed and the prefabricated whaleboat (transported disassembled in drays) be completed and launched. Local timber was also felled and utilised in building a second and smaller boat.

In sections of the Murray-Darling river system, rising waters frequently flood riverbank trees. This is a stretch of the Murray River near Loxton, South Australia.

At this point Sturt carefully selected provisions and crew, leaving a trusted man, Robert Harris, to return all else homeward and then await his return at Pondebadgery. On January 7, the boats headed downstream.

Fifteen miles westward lay a tributary stream which Sturt correctly judged to be the Lachlan River. Then came a series of misfortunes: the whaleboat was holed, the skiff was sunk (but salvaged) and irreplaceable items were stolen at night by Aborigines. Progress became difficult as extensive areas of dead timber and reeds obstructed the river. Relief came on January 14 as the journal records:

> "The men look anxiously out a-head; for the singular change in the river had impressed on them an idea, that we were approaching its termination; or near some adventure. On a sudden, the river took a general southern direction, but, in its tortuous corse swept round to every point of the compass with the greatest irregularity. We were carried at a fearful rate down its gloomy and contracted banks, and, in a moment of excitement, had little time to pay attention to the country through which we were passing … At 3 p.m., Hopkinson called out that we were approaching a junction, and in less than a minute afterwards, we were hurried into a broad and noble river."

Sturt's Desert Pea (Clianthus formosus) *is a striking example of Australia's distinctive flora. These vivid wildflowers bloom in South Australia's Flinders Ranges.*

Far Right:
Moon over Devils Marbles near Tennant Creek.

This "broad and noble" river was named the Murray River by Sturt, who was unaware it had previously been named the Hume by the Hume and Hovell expedition. Five days later they encountered seemingly hostile Aborigines, but Sturt and McLeay were ultimately able to make amiable contact with them. Four became particularly friendly.

On January 21, more Aborigines appeared and a bloody conflict seemed inevitable. Sturt wrote in his journal:

> "…I was determined to take deadly aim, in hopes that the fall of one man might save the lives of many. But at the moment, when my hand was on the trigger, and my eye was along the barrel, my purpose was checked by M'Leay…Turning around, I observed four men at the top of their speed…and in an incredibly short space of time [one of them] stood in front of the savage, against whom my aim had been directed. Seizing him by the throat, he pushed him backwards, and forcing all who were in the water upon the bank, he trod its margin with a vehemence and an agitation that were exceedingly striking."

The four Aboriginal men who had intervened and averted bloodshed proved to be those Sturt had befriended two days earlier. Amid this confusion, the confluence of a large northern river came into view. Sturt deduced this to be the Darling. Camp was made and cordial relations established with the Aborigines. The skiff, no longer needed, was burned and its copper sheathing distributed among the tribesmen. Significantly, all further contact with Aborigines downstream was peaceable.

The effects of folding forces and clear rock strata lines are both evident in the Elder Range formation in South Australia's Flinders Ranges region.

Thirty-three days downstream from the depot, the whaleboat entered a large shallow lake. Crossing this, Sturt located the choked rivermouth, and climbing an isthmus of sand, realised he was at the head of Encounter Bay. The expedition had achieved its goal.

Unable to contact a ship awaiting them at St Vincents Gulf, perilously short of provisions, and with scurvy rife among the party, Sturt's sole option was to row upstream to the depot and make contact with Harris waiting at Pondebadgery. The return trip was nightmarish, but the plan was successfully accomplished. Deprivation and exposure on the homeward journey caused one man to become insane and Sturt himself became seriously ill and blind for many months. The expeditioners returned to Sydney on May 25, 1830.

In Tasmania, as in New South Wales, settlement was steadily extending further afield, and colonial interest and the urge to explore focused attention on the west of the continent. Indirectly, the French were partly responsible for this. Since the First Fleet's arrival, the French had periodically made exploratory voyages, visiting several areas all around the Australian coastline. Officially, it was felt prudent to establish a British settlement on the western shores to forestall the possibility of French colonisation.

Therefore, when Captain James Stirling suggested an exploratory voyage to the Swan River, Governor Darling agreed. Stirling, board HMS *Success*, arrived off the Swan River on March 5, 1827. He conducted a thorough survey of the estuary and also led a party overland to a series of hills he named the Darling Range. From here, he saw and reported "an immense plain covered with forest". His report was well received by Governor Darling.

Returning to the Swan River in 1829, Captain Stirling fixed the sites of both Fremantle and Perth. The land was ripe for settlement and pioneers rapidly spread over the Darling Range and south to Bunbury, St Georges Sound and beyond Esperance Bay, establishing holdings.

The pellucid waters of The Labyrinth reflect the blue sky in Tasmania's Cradle Mountain-Lake St Clair National Park.

When John Oxley died in 1828, Governor Darling appointed Major (later Sir) Thomas Livingston Mitchell as Surveyor-General. Ambitious to explore, Mitchell was thwarted by Darling who ordered a general survey, bridge and road works and construction of an easier descent from the Blue Mountains. When Darling sailed for England, Mitchell proposed plans to acting governor Sir Patrick Lindesay, for an expedition to the northern rivers district, Lindesay agreed.

Inspired by the flimsy tales of a runaway convict about a great northern river, Mitchell set out on his first expedition. On November 24, 1831, he departed with a large expeditionary party. The present site of Tamworth, on the Peel River, was reached on December 11, and the party pressed on to the Namoi River close to the area explored by Cunningham four years earlier. A north-easterly route was chosen but progress was barred by the Nandewar Range.

On December 22, Mitchell established a depot on the Namoi river. Canvas boats were built to explore inland, but were quickly destroyed by underwater snags and valuable provisions were ruined or washed away.

An old eucalypt, known locally as Cazeaux's Tree, soars above plains abutting the folded ranges of Wilpena Pound in the Flinders Ranges, South Australia.

Far Right:
Lennard River in the Windjana Gorge National Park.

By New Year's Day 1832, the party rounded the foothills of the Nandewar Range and followed an almost northerly course across the plains. The Gwydir River was forded and correctly identified, and the party pressed north in appalling heat and on reduced rations.

On January 24, Mitchell discovered a large river which the Aborigines called Barwon. (It was the present day Macintyre River). Boats were ordered built. Mitchell surveyed downstream and found the confluence of the Gwydir River and saw also that waterborne travel was impractical. He concluded that all the northern rivers drained the same river basin and formed the headwaters of the Darling River.

The expedition was terminated; return being made imperative by hostile Aborigines, low rations, uncertain water supplies and the outbreak of scurvy among the men.

Mitchell returned to Sydney to find another Governor, Sir Richard Bourke, administering the colony. Bourke was disinclined to send his Surveyor-General out adventuring, until the British colonial Secretary, Viscount Goderich, suggested another attempt to trace the course of the Darling River. The task fell to Mitchell. Bourke ordered him to follow the Bogan River into the Darling and proceed downstream to determine whether it joined the Murray River. Mitchell, a believer in the inland sea concept, declared it did not.

Mitchell, again with a large and well-equipped expedition, left Boree in March 1935 to follow out his orders. There was drought throughout the district and he found the Bogan dry. Following its course he reached the Darling and built a stockade he named Fort Bourke. He intended this to be a depot and to proceed downstream in boats, but the falling river level precluded this and the entire party trekked downstream. Mitchell's party penetrated 480 kilometres, encountering increasing hostility from Aborgines as they progressed. Finally, a clash occurred close to the Menindee Lakes and several Aborigines were shot. Mitchell was forced to retreat 960 kilometres to Boree. Thus, the expedition failed in its major task.

Governor Bourke asked Mitchell to return to Menindee and to find exactly where the Darling River went. He left Orange on March 15, 1836, unaware that this third expedition was to bring him the triumph he so eagerly sought.

Mitchell was a controversial figure of complex character: considerate to subordinates and compassionate towards the convicts in this care, he was also self-assured, arrogant and autocratic, with a penchant to defy instructions if he felt it justified. On this expedition his chosen course was at variance with the Governor's instructions.

Wildflowers bestow a pinkish-mauve patina upon fields around Moralana Drive approaching the Wilpena Pound ranges in South Australia.

His first objective was Mount Granard north of the Lachlan River, from which he hoped to see a division between the Murray and Darling river valleys, vindicating his own theories concerning the rivers' courses. Unable to do so, he followed the Darling and arrived at Oxley's westernmost campsite on May 5.

His next objective was the Murrumbidgee River, which the expedition followed downstream to its junction with the Murray, arriving on May 23. Here Mitchell established a depot. On May 31, he sought and found the Darling River to the north-west, exploring upstream for twenty miles. To his chagrin his theories were disproven – but the true nature of the river system was revealed.

Returning to the depot, Mitchell now determined to trace the Murray towards its source. The party crossed to the western bank on June 13 and followed the river's course past the site of Swan Hill and also the Loddon River junction.

Mitchell ascended and named Mount Hope on June 28 to view the surrounding district, and here decided to abandon his instructions and strike out on a south-westerly course. His stated reason was: "The country which I have seen this day beyond Mount Hope, was too inviting to be left behind us unexplored; and I, therefore, determined to turn into it without further delay."

The expedition now crossed the Wimmera region, passed to the west of the Grampians mountain range, and made their way south-westwards towards the coast. Turning to the east-north-east brought them through rich and fertile plains. Leaving the main party, he detoured south with several men and on August 29, encountered the homestead of the Henty family. The Hentys had arrived by sea and settled the site over two years previously.

Sedges glow in late afternoon light and trees frame reflected images in the still waters of Lake Windermere in the Cradle Mountain-Lake St Clair National Park.

The homeward journey was slow as boggy ground delayed progress, but in mid-October the expedition reached the Murray River, north of modern day Wangaratta. From here his homeward route was roughly parallel to that taken by Hume and Hovell.

Mitchell's expedition had finally resolved the riddle of the rivers. It had also discovered vast areas of excellent country, accelerating the migration of pioneering graziers into Victoria, a process that had already begun.

Despite an 1829 'Limits of Location' proclamation by Governor Macquarie, settlement now began to outstrip organised exploration. Just as some landholdings in the nation's cradle – the Cumberland Plains around Sydney – had spread in an informal way, so too, other areas were being settled or 'squatted' on – as evidenced by Major Mitchell's encounter with the Henty family on their 'illegal' homestead at Portland Bay. By the 1820s, sealers, active in the Southern Ocean for years, had established a thriving settlement at Kangaroo Island. Settlements also existed in the Shoalhaven River, Monaro, Albury and New England districts as well as in Tasmania.

In 1835, John Batman and John Fawkner established Melbourne, and when Governor Bourke declared that Port Phillip district open for settlement in 1836, there were at least 200 squatters already settled within Victoria. In a similar case in the same year, when South Australia was declared a colony upon the arrival of Captain John Hindmarsh as the first Governor, it was evident that around 300 squatters had already established holdings. In 1839, the colonial administration gave de facto recognition to the squatting movement by dividing the area outside the 'Limits of Location' into nine squatting districts.

Still waters of the Northern Territory's Finke Gorge National Park perfectly mirror surrounding scrub and the rocky gorge walls.

There was now a jealous zeal to be the first to discover new farming land; both for prestige and profit. Controversy flared in 1840 when both 'Count' Paul Edmund de Strzelecki and Angus McMillan claimed discovery of the Gippsland area. Strzelecki, coming south over the Australian Alps, climbed and named Mount Kosciusko, Australia's highest peak. Further south he encountered a land holding established by McMillan. After becoming lost, Strzelecki finally reached Melbourne and reported the discovery of good lands. Mc Milton claimed prior discovery and had trekked and mapped the area extensively. Irrespective of the dispute, the area was rapidly settled.

The change of the decade saw most of the fertile districts discovered and fledgling cities established, and most exploration was now through more inhospitable terrain. A foretaste of what lay ahead was provided in 1837 when Lieutenant (later Sir) George Grey explored in north-western Australia. Speared by hostile Aborigines, facing starvation, thirst, exposure and the utmost adversity, Grey discovered the Glenelg and Gascoyne rivers. His long and agonising treks were fruitless though, for the land he traversed was arid, barren and desolate.

A rocky outcrop rears like some mediaeval citadel above a forest of pale dead timber, near Pelion East in the Cradle Mountain-Lake St Clair National Park.

Far Right:
Pinnacles of old rock protrude from later sand deposits in the desert area of the Nambung National Park in Western Australia.

The first major exploration of the 1840s was similar; enormous hardship endured and effort expended for negligible gain.

By mid-1840, Edward John Eyre, an experienced overlander, had already penetrated northward, discovering and naming Lake Torrens. He also probed westward to Streaky Bay and returning homeward, discovered the Gawler Range.

Both pastoralists and the government were anxious to break through the barrier of salt lakes hemming Adelaide's north and west. An expedition was proposed to determine if a stock route to Albany was practical. Eyre denounced this idea and suggested instead a trek northward beyond Lake Torrens and the Flinders Ranges in search of grazing lands. This suggestion was adopted and Eyre appointed to lead the expedition.

On June 18, Eyre took seven men, horses and provisions north to Mount Arden, where a depot was established. Eyre scouted ahead but the way north was blocked by desert and impassable saltpans. Several northern thrusts met saltpans and Eyre concluded that Adelaide was bounded to the north by an enormous and continuous horseshoe-shaped salt lake. Attempts were made to penetrate the Flinders Ranges but were repulsed by scorching heat and lack of water.

By February 1841 northward travel was abandoned and the expedition disbanded, but Eyre took the rash decision to attempt the first route proposed, and make westwards for Albany. He was accompanied by John Baxter and three Aborigines. Men and horses suffered terribly from thirst, exposure and fatigue. On April 29, two of the Aborigines murdered Baxter and fled, stealing most of the rations and water. Starvation and thirst now became major problems.

Eyre and Wylie, the remaining Aborigine, pressed onwards in desperate condition. Purely by remote chance, they encountered a whaling ship on June 2. Rested, reprovisioned and re-equipped by the whalers, the pair resumed their trek on June 14. They walked into Albany on July 7, to an enthusiastic welcome. The nightmarish trek covered over 1,600 kilometres, but academic interest aside, nothing had been accomplished.

Eyre's idea of a huge horseshoe lake created a myth that endured for a decade, but the earlier myth of the inland sea was about to be dispelled. The British colonial office approved an expedition to the geographical centre of the continent and appointed Charles Sturt as leader. He set out from Adelaide on August 15, 1844.

Folded rock strata display wave-like patterns on the exposed walls of the Hamersley Gorge and make stepped formations along the riverbed. The gorge cuts through the Hamersley Ranges.

To avoid Eyre's 'horseshoe lake', Sturt retraced his previous route along the Darling River to Menindee, then struck out to the north-west. He took sixteen men, horses, provisions and equipment, and confident an inland sea existed, a boat hauled by bullocks. Roughly 300 kilometres from Menindee, close to present day Milparinka, Sturt established a camp he named Depot Glen. Another 100 kilometres north, a second depot known as Fort Grey was built.

Northward travel was halted by a waterless, rock-strewn expanse now named Sturt's Stony Desert. Coopers Creek, discovered by the expedition, was rapidly drying out, making eastward travel impossible through lack of water. The only westward trek was halted at Lake Blanche, a dry saltpan.

The area was drought-stricken, and temperatures of 44°C by day dropping to −5°C at night caused severe hardship. Scurvy, thirst and starvation resulted in the death of one expeditioner and brought the others perilously close to the limits of human endurance.

The party struggled back to Adelaide on January 19, 1846. Sturt had trekked to within 240 kilometres of the continent's centre and disproved the inland sea theory.

The Olgas framed by mulga trees Ulura National Park World Heritage area.

The same year that Sturt began probing the continent's centre, Ludwig Leichhardt began a journey across its northern frontiers. This privately-sponsored expedition, despite attack by hostile Aborigines, inadequate provisioning and inept management, survived a wandering journey of nearly 5,000 kilometres from the Darling Downs to Port Essington on the north-west coast. Many rivers including the Isaac, Suttor, Burdekin, Lynd, Gilbert and Roper were discovered on this horrific trek. The survivors reached Port Essington on December 17, 1845 and sailed to Sydney, arriving in March 1846. By December, Leichhardt had assembled another party, and left the Condamine River to cross the continent from east to west. Eight months later they returned ill and half-starved, having covered 600 kilometres.

Leichhardt led a third expedition from Moreton Bay in 1848 to again attempt a continental crossing. None of this party were ever seen again and nothing certain is known of their fate, although several expeditions to find them, or relics of them, were mounted until well into the 1900s. These subsequent searches led to further exploration of hitherto unknown areas.

The turn of the decade brought tremendous changes to all facets of Australian society. By the end of 1850 a crisis was looming. The abolishment of convict

transportation, granting of representative government (albeit with an elitist bias), land tenure difficulties, and a depression especially affecting the wool industry were causing severe problems – grave enough to threaten the nation's growth. All these were, at least temporarily, totally overshadowed by an event which was to prove a catalyst for radical, pervasive and permanent change.

Crimson Rosellas in Queensland's Lamington National Park.

Far Right:
The lushness and diversity of tropical rainforests are clearly evident in this view from the Noah Range to the Daintree River estuary in Queensland.

This catalyst was the widespread discovery of gold. First discoveries were made in 1851 in New South Wales, with further strikes in Victoria later the same year. Goldrushes to various locations throughout the nation were to continue until the turn of the century. The effects were enormous and dramatic.

Population burgeoned explosively: in 1851 Australia had 437,665 people; in 1858 the country turned the first million mark, its second million in 1877, its third in 1889 and fourth in 1904. Initially commerce, agriculture, grazing and administrative work ground to a halt as virtually every able-bodied man left for the diggings. By December 1851 this situation was critical. La Trobe, Governor of Victoria, received a report reading:

"The postmaster apprehends an entire disruption of the business of his Department, unless remedial measures can be taken. The Surveyor-General is of a similar opinion. The Deputy-Registrar thinks that his subordinates will leave their occupation. The Superintendent of Police states that, though in accordance with authority he offered high rates of pay to his force, fifty out of fifty-five constables have determined to go to the gold-fields, but his clerk and chief constables will remain ... The Crown Solicitor apprehends complete embarrassment. The Denominational School Board fears loss of teachers ..."

Variegated bark colours lighten the shadows of a Karri forest near Pemberton in southern Western Australia.

As the goldfields developed and proliferated, wealth flooded into the country, commodities became scarcer and inflation escalated. Fortunately, public health remained good and law and order prevailed. Australia ceased to be predominantly penal and pastoral, and the influx of free middle class labour proved a powerful influence in establishing democracy. Ultimately, easily accessible alluvial gold petered out, and the capital intensive nature of deep lead mining led to the formation of speculative mining companies, and thence to the establishment of a stock exchange for scrip transactions.

The decline of the goldfields saw pastoral activity reinstated as the mainstay of the nation – but only after sweeping electoral and land tenancy reforms had all but demolished the huge squatting empires. Importantly, men had progressed from the enforced self-reliance of isolated bush life to the organised cooperation of the crowded diggings, resulting in a wages system and universal manhood suffrage. Vital social, political and financial structures were firmly in place, ensuring the nation's continued progress.

At first, goldrush activity centred in the south-east of the continent, but elsewhere the push to open new districts continued. Just prior to the change

Most Australian sand dunes are fixed, but in parts of the Nullarbor Plains barchans, or moving sand dunes, do occur. These barchans are in the Eucla National Park where winds give the sand mobility and pattern it with ripples.

of the decade, in 1848, Captain J. S. Roe opened up the Esperance Bay area of Western Australia, finding valuable pastoral lands, while Edmund Kennedy was far less fortunate. He and most of his party perished exploring Cape York. This decade saw Augustus Gregory, on two journeys in search of Leichhardt, extend knowledge of the northern areas, notably the central desert.

On August 20, 1860, amid considerable fanfare, a small expeditionary 'army' boasting horses, camels, carts, drays, eighteen men and twenty-one tonnes of provisions and equipment left Melbourne under the leadership of Robert O'Hara Burke. Their aim was to cross Australia from south to north.

Poor weather, long delays, financial worries and bickering marked the journey to Menindee on the Darling River, where a base camp was struck. On October 19, Burke and his second-in-command, William John Wills, took a small party from Menindee to build a depot at Coopers Creek. Instructions were left for the rest of the expedition to follow them.

Here, tired of awaiting the main party, aware that waterholes were drying up, and anxious to press northward, Burke decided to "dash into the interior and cross the continent at all hazards." Burke, Wills, King and Gray set out

Gnarled Hakea tree in the Western MacDonnell Ranges.

on December 16, instructing the Coopers Creek depot team to wait for three months or until rations ran out.

Burke's party made northwards for the Gulf of Carpentaria. Appalling heat necessitated night marches crossing Sturt's Stony Desert. Later, monsoons turned the land into a quagmire, hopelessly bogging the camels. Leaving King and Gray to tend them, Burke and Wills pressed on doggedly. On February 11, 1861, they reached a salty tidal stream; but mangrove swamps barred them from the ocean.

Starvation, thirst and exposure caused the death of Gray on the return journey. Burke, Wills and King reached the Coopers Creek depot on April 21 – just seven hours after the depot party had left. An attempt was made to reach a station at Lake Blanche, 240 kilometres west, but failed. Both Burke and Wills perished, but King was saved by sympathetic Aborigines. The continent had been crossed, but at a terrible cost.

The year 1860, in which the Burke and Wills expedition departed Melbourne, was also the year John McDouall Stuart began his attempts to cross from Adelaide to Australia's northern shores. Stuart had skirted the southern boundary of Lake Torrens and ridden north along its western flank to discover and name Chambers Creek. Returning via Streaky Bay to Adelaide, he organised a party to push overland to the Timor Sea. A base camp was established at Chambers Creek, and in March, Stuart and two companions set out.

Well northward, the Finke River was discovered and named, and a tremendous monolith Stuart encountered was called Chambers Pillar to honour a sponsor of the expedition. On April 22, on the northern slopes of the MacDonnell Ranges, Stuart's calculations convinced him that he was at the continent's geographical centre. He named a nearby hill Central Mount Sturt after fellow explorer Charles Sturt. This was later amended to Central Mount Stuart.

Probing further north he discovered the Tennant, Bonney, Bishop and Attack creeks. Here, water storage and hostile tribesmen forced a retreat to Adelaide. Another crossing was attempted by Stuart in June, but was defeated when waterless scrub plains were encountered 1,600 kilometres beyond Attack Creek.

His final, and successful, journey began on January 8, 1862, again from Chambers Creek. Hard riding brought them quickly to Newcastle Waters to confront the scrublands again. Casting about, they found a small creek which led through the scrub to rich grasslands beyond. A string of lakes was discovered and named Daly Waters and the sea was reached, east of the Adelaide River on July 24. Two days later the return trek began, made nightmarish by scurvy, thirst, food shortage and conflict with Aborigines. Adelaide was finally reached on December 17.

The transcontinental expeditions traversed arid and desolate regions, but fertile and accessible lands were revealed when Frank Gregory began a trek on the western coastline in 1861. He sought cotton-growing areas, as British cotton supplies were threatened by the American Civil War. Gregory discovered and named the Ashburton, Fortescue, De Grey and Oakover rivers, opening up 1,200,000 hectares of good grazing lands. He also discovered and named the Hamersley Range, now a major commercial resource of iron ore.

Storm clouds over The Brother's Chichester Range Pilbara.

In the same year, three separate search parties set out to determine the fate of the Burke and Wills expedition. Alfred William Howitt left Melbourne in June, and arriving at Coopers Creek on September 13, rescued King, the sole survivor of the dash northwards with Burke. On a subsequent visit to Coopers Creek, Howitt retrieved the bodies of Burke and Wills for burial in Melbourne.

Meanwhile John McKinlay headed north from Adelaide to Coopers Creek. He found Gray's body. Flash flooding and conflict with Aborigines forced him north to the Gulf of Carpentaria. Like Burke, McKinlay was barred from the sea by mangroves. Turning east, the rescue party struggled through to a homestead west of Port Dennison, now called Bowen. Another trail had become known.

One man who speculated that Burke and Wills may have headed east into Queensland was William Landsborough. His course was to make for the Albert River on the Gulf of Carpentaria by sea. From here he led two treks to the south-west, searching for signs of Burke, until at a station on the Warrego River he heard the news of Howitt's success and King's rescue. In the course of his journeys he had discovered good lands, including the fertile Barkly Tableland.

Speculation was also still current concerning Leichhardt's fate. When Duncan McIntyre left the Paroo River in 1865, to examine the country westward and around the Gulf of Carpentaria, interest in Leichhardt was reawakened by the discovery of two trees marked with an 'L'. Four years later, John Forrest took an expedition inland from near Perth, to search unsuccessfully for traces of Leichhardt's trail. Both expeditions crossed hitherto unknown areas.

An important step in opening the continental interior was taken in 1870 when construction began on the Overland Telegraph, which followed John McDouall Stuart's route. Completed in 1972, this vital communications link also became an important base for exploration.

In this decade, exploration centred mainly in the north and west of the continent. On April 15, 1873, a large expedition on camelback left Alice Springs led by Colonel Peter Warburton. The aim of this expedition was to traverse the country between Central Mount Stuart and Perth.

A massive Red Gum leans towards Coopers Creek, near Innamincka in northern South Australia. Eucalyptus are only found at favoured sites in this arid, Acacia-dominated country. This tree is close to the depot site of the ill-fated Burke and Wills expedition.

Water shortage and starvation forced abandonment of this goal, and after a horror trek of over 3,000 kilometres, the party ultimately struggled to the Oakover River on the north-west coast. So severe was this journey that many of the camels were eaten by the expeditioners in their bid to survive.

Eight days after Warburton's departure, William Grosse led another expedition out of Alice Springs. This party explored westward of the MacDonnell Range for 1,400 kilometres and found good grazing near the Musgrave Range. Grosse also discovered and named the world's largest monolith, Ayers Rock (now know as its Aborginal name Uluru). In this same year Ernest Giles began an expedition to find a route overland from Central Australia to the western coast. This journey, another horror trek, was unsuccessful in achieving its aim but a great deal of new territory was charted. One feature found, and named for a dead comrade, was the Gibson Desert.

Giles was not deterred, and was to achieve a double crossing of the western half of the continent in 1875. He left Beltana in South Australia on May 6, using camels to cross the arid wastelands, and arrived in Perth on November 10. He left Perth on January 13, to return. North of Perth he reached the

Murchison River and then headed east, arriving at the Overland Telegraph on August 3, 1876. These journeys added greatly to the store of knowledge of the central area's geography.

Late in the decade, Alexander Forrest undertook a series of exploratory journeys which opened up the Kimberley Ranges districts. On July 24, 1879, he discovered and named the Ord River. This area was rapidly settled.

By the 1880s, barely a century after the arrival of the First Fleet, virtually all major exploration was completed. Surveyors and others were still to 'fill the gaps' by penetrating minor new districts; charting river courses, establishing homesteads and townships, clearing stock routes and planning railroads. This is the process of expansion and pioneering; distinct from exploration. It is to the explorers that the credit must go for first shedding light on the unknown; often at the cost of extreme hardship or death. These stubborn, determined men – whether their motives were purist or pragmatic – well deserve the appellation 'hero'.

Wangi Falls in the Litchfield National Park.

Australia can broadly be described as being big, flat, dry and old.

It is big by any standard of measurement used. The land area of 7,692,024 square kilometres is almost as great as that of the U.S.A. (excluding Alaska and Hawaii), about 50 per cent greater than Europe and roughly 32 times greater than that of the U.K. It is ranked as the sixth largest country in the world. From the westernmost point to the easternmost extremity is about 4,000 kilometres. From the northern tip to the southernmost point on the mainland is 3,180 kilometres, and to the southern extremity of Tasmania, 3,680 kilometres. The coastline, including Tasmania, stretches for over 35,500 kilometres.

It is the flattest of all countries. The lowest point is within Lake Eyre, 15 metres below sea-level, while the highest point is Mount Kosciusko which reaches 2,228 metres above sea-level – quite low by global standards. Within this narrow vertical band of only 2,243 metres, a broad spectrum of landforms exists.

It is a predominantly dry place, the driest of all continents except Antarctica. One third of the land is arid desert. In proportion to its area, Australia has the lowest precipitation and run-off of all continents.

It is also the driest in terms of precipitation to run-off ratio; over 85 per cent of naturally occurring water is lost by evapo-transpiration. To compound the problem, the precipitation that does occur, does so very unevenly – 80 per cent of all run-off comes from little over a quarter of the total land area.

It is very, very old. Throughout Australia the generally rounded and eroded landforms attest to the continent's antiquity. Unlike Europe and North America, where many of the landforms date back 20,000 years to when the great ice sheets retreated, the age of landforms in Australia is generally measured in so many *millions* of years. Indeed, some of the rock formations of the Western Plateau are known to be over 3,000 million years old, and are considered the world's oldest.

The overall shape of the landmass is best defined by the continental shelf, rather than the coastline which has varied with fluctuations in the sea-level occurring through the aeons. In profile, the continent is divided into three broad zones – the Western Plateau, the Central Lowlands and the Eastern Highlands, of which Tasmania is a part. The profile is broad but very narrow vertically, similar to a wide saucer.

As the moon rises, the last rays of sunlight bring warm colour to Chambers Pillar, an enormous monolith in the desert of the Northern Territory.

While the general shape of Australia has been caused by major earth movements, most surface detail is the result of both water and wind erosion. Fully a third of the continent drains inland, and the rivers, while they may be eroding valleys near their highland sources, are also filling their long lower courses with alluvium. Most such rivers are very ancient. External drainage to the sea occurs around the western, northern and eastern coastlines. Typically, this external drainage is by shorter, younger and more vigorous rivers. A notable exception is the Murray-Darling river system, the only drainage from the central area to the sea.

Much of Australia's interior is semi-arid or arid, with sand deserts or gibber plains ('gibbers' are small stones), and dry saltpans which intermittently fill to become salt lakes. Sand dunes are common and are now mostly fixed, longitudinally aligned along dominant wind directions. Aridity seems to be a geologically young phenomenon, as no dunes or saltpans are older than a million years.

Other factors which have influenced landforms have been glaciation in Permian times (about 300 million years ago) and also the Quaternary ice ages (within the past 2 million years) as well as marine inundation which occurred in the Cretaceous period (about 140 million years past).

An eroded sandstone shelf at Boy Martin Point, Royal National Park.

Far Right:
The stony nature of the arid Flinders Ranges is clearly evident in this view from Sillers Lookout, near Arkaroola. Foreground plants are young grasstrees; older specimens usually sprout atop fire-blackened trunks.

At this time Australia was already low and flat, and rising seas invaded the interior, dividing the land into three separate areas. More recently in the Tertiary period (about 3 million years ago), volcanoes erupted in eastern

Australia, laying down huge lava plains. It was also in this period that the Eastern Highlands were uplifted.

The outline of the continental shelf results mainly from the pattern of break-up of Gondwanaland – a supercontinent which included Australia, Africa, Antarctica and many island fragments – about 300 million years ago. Separation of the Australian continental mass occurred about 55 million years ago and was followed by a roughly northerly drift. The continental shelf is generally broad and is bounded by a steep continental slope, gouged into submarine canyons off South Australia. It is very narrow off the New South Wales coast but spreads to form a wide plateau off Queensland. It is here that the Great Barrier Reef has formed for the past two million years.

Rises in sea-level, as recently as 6,000 years ago separated Tasmania and New Guinea from the mainland. The geographic features of today are the result of a long-continued process of disturbance and erosion, in a unique setting, giving rise to landscapes typically and distinctly Australian in character.

Snow patches, rock ridges and boggy alpine meadows form a backdrop to a small tarn at Charlotte Pass in the Kosciusko National Park. This is the area where Australia's lowest-ever temperature of –22°C was recorded.

As Australia extends from roughly latitude 10°S to 44°S it experiences a broad range of climatic conditions; the one-third of the continent north of the Tropic of Capricorn falls within the tropical zone, while the southern two-thirds lie in the temperate zone. However, Australia's relatively isolated global position and generally low geography have the effect of ameliorating the severe climatic extremes found within similar-sized landmasses elsewhere. The only geographical feature to affect atmospheric airstreams is the Eastern Highlands; and resultant changes to not extend far.

Despite Australia's general climatic moderation, temperature and rainfall maxima and minima cover a fairly broad band. The maximum temperature recorded in Australia was 53.0°C at Cloncurry in Queensland during 1889, and the minimum was –23°C recorded at Charlotte Pass in the Southern Alps during 1994. Rainfall shows similar diversity: the north-east coast between Cairns and Cardwell has the highest annual rainfall with some areas averaging over 8,000 mm per year, more than 80 times that of the driest townships in northern South Australia.

Spanning these particular latitudes brings Australia's northern and southern areas within the area of influence of two major global weather systems: the

Low rounded headlands embay the sea near Esperance, Western Australia.

tropical monsoons and the Roaring Forties latitudinal windbelt, both of which fluctuate slightly northwards and southwards on a seasonal basis. This results in the northern areas of Australia experiencing a hot, rainy season in summer (November to April) as warm, moist monsoonal air invades from equatorial regions. Fine, warm weather is typical in the south during this time.

Conversely, during winter (May to October) the southernmost areas come under the influence of the cold air directed northwards by intense depressions in the Southern Ocean. A series of these depressions follow the path of the westerly windbelt, bringing cold, wet winters. At these times northern Australia is fine and dry.

Between these northern and southern areas is a hot, dry inland desert. Here, drought is a common occurrence due primarily to high atmospheric pressures, the distance from the sea and the absence of high mountains. Average rainfall is less than 200 mm. Within this area, daytime temperatures are high for prolonged periods, but as there is no cloud cover, heat dissipates rapidly at night and temperatures are low. At Alice Springs the daily minimum at dawn in July is typically 3.8°C, whereas the mid-afternoon maximum is 20.0°C; a daily temperature range of 16.2°C.

Climate is modified on the eastern seaboard by the presence of the Eastern Highlands. Here rainfall is generally more prolific than elsewhere on the continent, as clouds are formed within moist air that flows in from the Pacific Ocean and is forced to rise by mountains.

Numerous ferntrees thrive in the moist conditions created by waterfalls. This is the beautiful Russell Falls cascading over near-horizontal rock strata at Mount Field National Park in Tasmania.

Several factors contribute to the pattern of Australia's natural vegetation distribution: rainfall, temperature, soil type and, in a limited context, altitude. Most important by far is rainfall. Thus vegetation zones closely follow rainfall patterns; although considerable local variations can occur within them.

In northern monsoonal areas, along both flanks of the Eastern Highlands, in Tasmania and in the south-western districts receiving rain from the moist Westerlies, water is plentiful. Here, fertile soils and abundant rainfall give rise to a variety of forests. Inland, where rainfall is less frequent, the forests give way to scrublands. These persist in a broad but disjointed swathe across both the north and south of the continent and along most of the eastern edge of the Central Lowlands, generally defining the semi-arid areas.

Within the more barren and truly arid central areas of the continent, three vegetation zones exist. Hummock grasses predominate in the west, tussock grasses prevail in the east, and in the pockets of stony desert where soil is very meagre, short-lived herbaceous saltbushes and burrs appear briefly after the infrequent rains. In terms of area, the scrublands and grasslands are largest, consistent with Australia's chiefly hot and dry climate.

The scrublands consist of saltbrush, bluebrush, gorses, tall wiry grasses and heaths, with an upper cover of tall woody shrubs and small trees less than 10 metres tall. The density of this upper cover may vary from as low as 10 per cent to as high as 70 per cent from location to location. The scrub itself varies similarly, from sparse and readily passable to dense and impenetrable.

A Pandanus Palm creates a stark silhouette in the glowing sunset near Noosa on Queensland's southern coast.

Hummock grasses are typically low and spiky grass species, commonly referred to collectively as 'spinifex'. Occasionally they grow as an understorey and where shrubs are absent, such as on very sandy plains or sand-ridge deserts, the hummock grasses become the dominant vegetation over vast areas. These grasses seldom achieve a ground cover density of more than 10 to 30 per cent.

Tussock grass species are more compact in form and require slightly higher nutrient levels than hummock grasses. Consequently, they grow mainly on the floodplains of such non-perennial watercourses as the Finke, Georgina and Diamantina rivers, or about Coopers Creek and the abutting channel country. They occasionally achieve ground cover densities of up to 70 per cent, and may be accompanied by a very sparse cover of saltbush and bluebush.

Within the arid areas, both scrubland and grassland, isolated specimens or small stands of dryland adapted larger trees appear. These include such types as Baobab (*Adansonia gregorii*), Desert Oak (*Casuarina decaisneana*), Belah (*Casuarina cristata*) and Bottle Tree (*Brachychiton rupestre*), each with a particular range of occurrence.

By far the greatest diversity is found within the forested zone. Forests are classified into three general types: low forest, tall forest and closed forest. Because of their locations, closed forests are sometimes also called 'rainforests'.

Pale trunked eucalypts grow in the bed of the Finke River in the Western MacDonnell Ranges of the Northern Territory. Behind severely eroded rock outcrops are the typical forms of a folded range.

Low forests are easily the most extensive and widespread, occupying most of the fertile and moderately well watered areas. Trees vary from 10 to 30 metres in height, establishing cover densities of 10 to 70 per cent. It is in these forests that most of the five to six hundred species of eucalypts are found, although their individual species distribution varies widely. Typically, trees are well mingled in a low forest, either with individual specimens of a particular species dispersed or occurring in several established stands. Moister areas tend to be fairly well monopolised by varied eucalypts. In drier areas, eucalypts may be partially or almost entirely displaced by species such as Brigalow (*Acacia harpophylla*), Mulga (*Acacia aneura*), Cyprus Pine (*Callitris*) or Belah (*Casuarina cristata*). Understoreys contain a profuse variety of bushes, shrubs, heaths and grasses, and range from sparse to thick.

Tall forests occur in pockets along the southern portion of the Eastern Highlands, in Tasmania, and in Australia's south-western corner. The upper storey is dominated by eucalypts exceeding 30 metres in height and providing a cover density of between 10 and 70 per cent. Species vary; Karri (*Eucalyptus diversicolor*) and Jarrah (*Eucalyptus marginata*) spread over substantial areas in the south-west but are not found in the east where Mountain Ash (*Eucalyptus regnans*) is often the most common species. In most tall forests, one eucalypt species is clearly the most commonly found, although several other eucalypts and members of other genera are mingled throughout. Understorey vegetation is widely diverse; smaller trees, woody shrubs, treeferns, bracken, heaths, ferns, herbaceous plants and fungi all usually appear. The main determinants for these are soil depth, soil fertility and the amount of available sunlight.

Ghost Gums and rock walls in Trephina Gorge in the East MacDonnell Ranges, Northern Territory.

Closed forest only occurs in pockets where rich fertile soils receive a rainfall great than 1,200 mm per annum. Trees grow from 10 to 30 metres tall, establishing cover densities well in excess of 70 per cent, thus permitting little sunlight to penetrate. Such forests are notable for their dense growth and the absence of the ubiquitous eucalypts. Some trees, such as those of the *Ficus* group, are banyans, sending out aerial roots adventitiously to the ground, enabling the tree to spread over a wide area. Typically, poor light penetration limits the development of a dense understorey, but small herbaceous plants, ferns, mosses, lichens and fungi all manage to survive. Epiphytic and parasitic plants often grow on trunks and branches. Within this midstorey vines, ferns and orchids are frequently evident.

It should be borne in mind that all of the foregoing descriptions of major vegetation zones represent only the very broadest categorisation. Considerable differences occur within each zone according to local conditions such as latitude, altitude, soil type, soil fertility, temperature, wind exposure, salinity and other factors. For these reasons, the descriptions given should not be treated as being precisely definitive of particular vegetative groupings.

Clearly, closed forests in tropical settings will differ to those in Tasmania. Although they share common characteristics, each will likely be different in species, habit and appearance.

Other wide variations in plants exist throughout Australia. Most are the result of specialised adaptation to the specific demands of a particular habitat, and hence do not belong in any geographically-based grouping. Swamps, riversides, alpine areas, tidal zones and other particular habitats all produce distinctive plant types. Many have evolved in isolation and are uniquely Australian, or indeed, unique to one locality.

Two of the Devils Marbles balance precariously near Wauchope in the Northern Territory. These rocks resulted from the breaking of a granite mass into rectangular blocks. Subsequent flaking and erosion has produced these spheroidal forms.

Far Right:
Fanned clouds Elephant Rocks at William Bay National Park.

Australian landscapes are manifestly different to those of other countries, and geographical, geologic and climatic factors aside, the difference is attributable to quite evidently disparate vegetation. This results largely from the very high proportion of endemic plants, of all types and sizes, occurring within natural plant groupings. Thus, it is common for Australia's flora to be labelled 'unique'; but this imprecise description is not strictly true. Members of most of the world's large plant families appear throughout Australia, sometimes in forms commonly occurring elsewhere on the globe. Conversely, locally common and 'typically Australian' genera, like *Acacia* and *Eucalyptus*, occur naturally in Africa and tropical America, and in the Indonesian Archipelago, respectively. Therefore, despite the high ratio of endemic plant species, to call Australia's flora unique is to make a dubious claim which is clearly a matter of degree.

In common with other southern hemisphere floras, the Australian flora has temperate flowering trees that are evergreen rather than deciduous, and also shares a conspicuous absence of dominant conifers. But a marked difference from other southern continental floras persists. What then, is typical of Australian plant communities and bestows upon them their distinctively Australian character?

*Near Echidna Chasm in the
Bungle Bungle National Park.*

The first step in answering this is to decide what is typical. Both the hummock and tussock grasslands, while large in extent, are atypical in their lack of aerial cover and their sparsity. Both closed forests and alpine areas only occur in a few relatively small and isolated pockets. This leaves scrublands, low forests and tall forests. These are extensive and share well-developed ground covers with the addition of overhead cover, and such commonality may be called 'typical'. All may be termed bushlands, or in more popular parlance, 'the Australian bush'.

The Australian bush is distinguished by the fact that two large genera, *Eucalyptus* and *Acacia*, between them, clearly dominate almost all the plant associations in the continent. These are the most common denominator – truly the 'backbone of the bush'. In defining the typical or distinctive nature of the Australian flora then, it may generally be stated that it is composed of plant communities dominated by *Eucalyptus* or *Acacia* species, but includes representatives of diverse genera and species which do not occur anywhere else. Both of these major genera, *Eucalyptus* and *Acacia*, merit further examination.

Eucalyptus is undoubtedly the most significant Australian plant genus, both biologically and physically. The genus includes between five and six hundred species which vary in habit, range and distribution, and a significant proportion of these species could be classed as uncommon. Eucalyptus are hardwoods which characteristically occur in both low forests and tall forests, according to species distribution, and vary in both ground cover density and aerial cover density from thick to open. Only a few species have been successful in populating closed forest margins or alpine areas, despite an evident preference for moister habitats. They are relatively few in arid and even semi-arid areas, and with rare exceptions, are confined to favourable situations such as stream lines and rock outcrops where moisture is more readily available.

While not quite as overwhelmingly significant as *Eucalyptus*, the genus *Acacia* is also enormously successful, and with over eight hundred species, is Australia's most diversified genus. *Acacia* occurs in several forms in Africa and tropical America, but one characteristic section of the genus, *Phyllodinae*, dominates the Australian representation and is overwhelmingly endemic to the region. The *Acacia* species appear in nearly all plant communities, including closed forests, but in a minor way. They rise to community dominance, displacing *Eucalyptus* in the openly wooded floras of arid and semi-arid areas. Oddly,

Palm trees stand regally above a shallow and narrow beach at Port Douglas in northern Queensland.

only 14 per cent of the species inhabit very arid central areas, while 40 per cent are represented in Australia's moister south-western corner. This may be partly due to the separation of eastern and western botanical provinces by the invasion of central Australia by the sea during the Miocene epoch, but appears to indicate a species preference towards a more Mediterranean climate. The *Acacia* species adaptability and range cause them to frequently mingle with eucalypts in many situations. The Golden Wattle (*Acacia pycnantha*) has been adopted as Australia's national flower, and this well known species is illustrative of the general form of most of Australia's *Acacia* population.

Considering the disparate general ranges of Eucalyptus and Acacia, the idea of typical Australian bush must been seen as a multifaceted concept. Plant associations may be dominated by either of these genera or they may mingle. Local conditions of aridity and soil type will determine major genera ratios, overall densities and which particular species are present. This will also hold true for the constituent genera and species of the accompanying understorey.

The silvery cascades of McKenzie Falls lighten a sombre rock wall in Victoria's Grampians Range.

Far Right:
The power of the Snowy River has sculpted hard granite into strange forms at Kosciuzko National Park.

GORGE

Hemmed by rock walls tall and steep,
Darkling pools old secrets keep.
Crystal clear and mirror calm,
Reflecting sky, scrub, gum and palm.
Reflecting too, on ages past,
When turbid torrents strong and fast
Carved raw rock chasms deep and vast
And raging rapids crashed and hewed
Relentlessly these ranges through
As from the flooded plains they spewed.

This fissured breach gouged long ago
By ancient river's timeless flow,
Now hosts moss, grass, fern and tree
Springing 'twixt the scattered scree,
To form a haven, moist and green,
A habitat for life between
Cool earth and heaven's scorching sheen.
This refuge from the desert's heat
Now eches to the rhythmic beat
Of shy marsupials' swift retreat.

The work of countless ages done
Now shelters life from searing sun.
So pause a while, in contemplation,
Of nature's cycles of creation.

Fracture planes show clearly
in the blocky rock walls of
the Katherine Gorge.

Beyond the bushlands, the arid zone also warrants attention. Australia's deserts are unmatched in extent by any other deserts south of the Equator and differ from other deserts in that very few succulents or conspicuous cacti are present. There are a few drought resistant woody plants in the arid zone, but the flora of the region is overwhelmingly composed of small shrubs and grasses. This area has a unique combination of cosmopolitan and endemic plants; some very ancient and many quite fragile and unable to withstand pastoral activity. During the long dry periods most plants show little visual difference, leading to an impression that the plains are fairly uniformly clad. Following rains however, this impression is quickly dispelled as the low growing plants burst into bloom in vivid colours and astonishing variety. Indeed, the Australian arid zone flora is one of the most diverse and prolific in the world, although it is characterised by very small and specific distributions of many plant types.

Another plant environment, very different but equally harsh, is found in alpine areas. Australia's alpine areas are confined to pockets atop the Eastern Highlands and experience freezing winters, high summer temperatures and extreme wind exposure. Above the tree line particularly, the alpine flora consists of a rare combination of ancient southern plants and less ancient adapted Australian ones. Because of wind exposure and wide seasonal temperature variation, plants tend to be low growing and characterised by relatively short growing periods. Australian alpine areas are remarkable for their very low tree lines. This is brought about by a general lack of frost-hardy trees, and the scarcity of conifers in particular. *Eucalyptus* commonly occurs above the snow line but is modified into low and massive forms to withstand snow loading.

Stalactites hang as stalagmites slowly grow to form limestone pillars in the Jewel Cave. Limestone caves occur in several Australian localities; this one is in the south-west of Western Australia.

Undoubtedly the flora of the closed forests is the most ancient, and has been the most influential of all Australian plant groups. Temperate and subtropical closed forests occur in a number of isolated pockets along the coast and ranges of both Tasmania and the mainland. They are the surviving remnants of the very ancient Gondwanan flora which entirely covered Australia when it was still connected to Antarctica sixty million years ago. These residues of primitive floristic stocks are the bases from which most of the contemporary Australian flora has evolved. Here dwell Antarctic Beech (*Nothofagus*) species, and taxa which have experienced the least evolutionary change, including some of the world's most primitive genera of flowering plants. From these Gondwanan stocks of the closed forests – periodically invaded by cosmopolitan biotica, and modified by adaption to great geographical and climatic changes of the distant past – has arisen the great variety of genera and species which comprise the bulk of the Australian flora of today.

London Bridge near Port Campbell formation after its collapse.

ooking at Australian vegetation as a whole on a non-zonal basis, it is evident that it is a distinctive botany, markedly different from that of corresponding northern latitudes. The dominant genus, *Eucalyptus* is evergreen and characterised by usually narrow, flat and pendulous leaves, quite unlike the broader, upright leaves which are common to many of the deciduous temperate trees of the northern hemisphere. Among other common genera such as *Acacia*, *Casuarina* and *Banksia*, small leaved foliage is common, and this is true of most understorey plants also, such as many *Leptospermum*, *Epacris* and *Boronia* species.

Most foliage is of a relatively dull green except among plants of moist tropical habitats. However, especially among plants from dry habitats, great textural variety exists and a distinctive silvery-grey leaf colouration occurs. The *Cassia*, *Eremophila* and *Acacia* genera all have species displaying this characteristic. Reddening of foliage is also common, not so much as a prelude to the shedding of leaves as it is an indication of new growth. This occurs with many *Eucalyptus* species, *Syzygium luehmannii*, *Nothofagus moorei* and many others. Reddening of leaves occurs as a seasonal variation too, signalling the onset of winter, as with *Allocasuarina torulosa* and some *Leptospermum* species. Flowers

similarly show variance with northern hemisphere counterparts. In Europe and North America, seasons are more definite and flowering is a relatively rare occurrence in winter; in Australia, although this pattern holds generally true, the seasons merge more gradually and the flowering of *Crowea*, *Correa* and *Banksia* species can commonly persist throughout the autumn and winter. A distinguishing characteristic of Australian flowers is their great diversity of shape. Although broad, open-petalled and upright flowers do occur, they are not at all prevalent.

Stalactites form 'veil' and 'wedding cake' formations in King Solomons Cave in northern Tasmania.

Far Right:
The aptly named Remarkable Rocks are wind-eroded boulders on an exposed headland of Flinders Chase National Park on South Australia's Kangaroo Island. Here the setting sun accentuates their strange configurations.

This may be the result of reliance on pollinators other than bees. Bees are major pollinators in the northern hemisphere but have a lesser role in Australia. Native bees exist in Australia, but plants tend to rely more on birds, small aboreal mammals, other insects and wind. Thus, closed flower forms suited to the bills of nectar-seeking birds, or brush-like flowers open to winds from all directions are common.

Common shapes of Australian wildflowers are tubular, brushy, globular, pea-flower or daisy-like forms. Typical of the tubular group are *Boronia*, *Correa*, *Billardiera* and *Styphelia* genera. Open, brush-like blooms are found on *Banksia*, *Grevillea*; and *Telopea*, commonly known as 'Waratahs' which are a sub-group of the *Proteaceae*. Globular forms can be composite as in *Acacia* (wattles) or discrete as in some *Melaleuca* or *Eucalyptus* species. Pea-flowering genera including *Bossiaea*, *Oxylobium*, *Hovea* and others, while the daisy-like group is represented by genera such as *Olearia* and species within *Helipterum*, *Helichrysum* and *Brachycome*.

Much finer differentiation continues within these broad classifications, and enormous variety exists – but that is beyond the intended scope of this description. Clearly, the Australian flora is botanically complete and fully developed, with no ecological niche left unoccupied.

Establishment of the Australian flora chronologically preceded the establishment of the similarly distinctive and diverse native fauna, although these two elements paralleled their development through millennia, to arrive at full ecological integration many thousands of years ago. The Australian fauna has several unique creatures, as well as cosmopolitan elements among migratory birds and widespread marine species. Some animals, such as the monotremes and marsupials, represent early stages of mammalian evolution, possibly as a result of geographic isolation, and are unknown elsewhere on the globe. For whatever cause, animal evolution in Australia has produced a fauna with unique characteristics.

One such characteristic is a preponderance of vegetation animals and an absence of large and dangerous predators. Intra-ecological predation occurs, but is primarily confined to small animals. Animals dangerous to man are broadly limited to reptilian and insect forms inland, although several forms of potentially lethal marine animals are to be found along the coasts.

A skeleton of dry twigs protrudes from a red sand dune in the Northern Territory desert.

Far Right:
Everlastings on Mr Howitt Alpine National Park.

Frequently, a distinctive feature of Australian landscapes is the presence of old and eroded geographical forms, or geological remnants exposed by ancient erosion processes. These features may be broad in extent, such as the rugged edge of an old escarpment dominating a wide panorama, or localised forms such as monoliths or volcanic plugs. To understand the occurrence of such distinctive features involves an appreciation of the geological-geographical processes that produced them. Geology is the study of rocks and their formation, and this, because of the nature of the genesis of rocks, includes the historical study of geography, since all geographical formation results from geological activity.

Ultimately, all rocks are derived from the molten and elemental material of the planet itself. However, they are classified into three types – igneous rocks, usually very hard and of crystalline composition, which solidified from molten crustal material; sedimentary rocks, laid down from materials eroded from older rock by the action of wind, water or ice; and metamorphic rocks, which have become crystalline through alteration by heat and pressure. The ancient Gondwanan supercontinent, of which Australia is one fragment, contained all three types and all are represented in Australia today.

Most rock volumes within Australia formed during Precambrian times and the Palaeozoic era, an immense time span stretching from the beginnings of earth history about 4,500 million years past to around 235 million years ago; still a very ancient time. Simplistically stated, Australia is composed of a broad Precambrian shield, disrupted to the east by the Tasman Geosyncline, and overlaid by relatively younger rocks. Although the continent is composed chiefly of these very ancient materials, little of the present surface is as old as that. Those few Precambrian surfaces that exist now have been exposed by the erosion of younger overlying rocks.

Waterlilies spread on the surface of a Melaleuca *rimmed billabong near the Adelaide River in the Northern Territory.*

Much of the fundamental shaping of Australia's profile took place in Permian times, about 250 million years ago. Most areas had previously been torn and twisted by intense tectonic action as the earth's crustal plates moved, but the last strong movements, which crumpled the sea-floor and created high submarine mountain ranges, occurred in this period. Inland, this tectonic movement raised mountains in south-eastern Queensland and the New England area, but since the process stopped early, Australia lacks extensive areas of young folded mountains. Also in Permian times, great ice sheets invaded in the form of titanic glaciers, generally scraping land areas down.

Following this Permian glaciation, water run-off, alluvial deposition and gravitational slope processes reduced the Gondwanan area to lands of low relief. There were some places, like the Great Artesian Basin of central Australia, which were bent gently downwards. These were progressively filled by rivers, lakes and swamps during the Mesozoic era, roughly 235 million years past. Later, towards the end of the Jurassic period (around 135 million years ago), Australia began to separate from Antarctica as part of the fragmentation of Gondwanaland. This caused dolerite, an igneous rock, to well up between the sedimentary rock strata of Tasmania as intrusive sills. This dolerite now caps many Tasmanian plateaus.

During the Cretaceous period (130 to 70 million years past) the sea invaded much of Australia, particularly the Central Lowlands. However, traces of unsubmerged land still survive as upland erosion surfaces cutting across the ancient rocks. Several extensive shallow valley systems originated at this time and are still in evidence in areas of the Western Plateau. Towards the end of the Cretaceous period, separation of Australia and Antarctica accelerated, opening up the Tasman Sea. Final disconnection of the two land masses was completed around 55 million years ago, causing Australia to begin a long northward tectonic drift.

Drift was halted about 20 million years ago in the Tertiary period when the Australian crustal plate impacted upon the Pacific crustal plate, creation the fold mountains of New Guinea, and accelerating the emergence of the Central Lowlands and marginal basins of the Western Plateau from the sea. At this point Australia was in its present position straddling the Tropic of Capricorn, and experiencing a warm and wet climate. Deep weathering of the rocks took place throughout the continent, giving rise to lateritic soil profiles rich in iron and subject to silica deposition.

View across Mulga Trees to Mount Connor.

This Tertiary period (65 to 2 million years past) saw widespread hewing of the continent's physical landscape. In the west, the deeply weathered profiles over the Western Plateau were extensively etched away, but formed sharply broken and hard crusts on flat topped ranges. Ridges of substantially harder rock, such as the MacDonnell Ranges, were eroded into gorges by river action. In the Exmouth Gulf region, compression forces created low folded ranges. Eastward, generalised uplift was already elevating the continental boundary, and this was accentuated by prolonged upwarping along the length of the Eastern Highlands. Plateaus at various levels resulted, some sectioned by deep gorges. In the south, faulting caused the depression of the South Australian Gulfs and elevated the Flinders and Lofty Ranges, which were then cut and scoured by rivers. The Great Victorian Valley, extending from Warrnambool to Gippsland, was bent and depressed, as was the Bass Strait area. These major earth movements were accompanied by volcanic activity, both eruptive and intrusive, extending from the Atherton Tablelands through to Western Victoria and south into Tasmania.

Evening mists descending on Lake Pedder, a World Heritage listed area of Tasmania's south-west.

Far Right:
Man's imprint dominates this view of rolling hills in the potato-growing district of Hallston, in Victoria's Strzelecki Ranges. Roads and fences crisscross the landscape and imported trees are regimented into windbreaks.

COOL RAINFOREST

Through cool valleys' forested gloom,
In emerald light, old treeferns loom,
Brackens round their bases sprawl,
Upon their trunks fern tendrils crawl,
From the forest's littered floor,
Enriched by mould and seed and spore,
Mighty beeches upward soar;
Wide-spreading branches sheltering all,
Layering ground with thick leaf fall.

Scattered shafts of sunlight slope,
Clinging vines through thickets grope,
Needled sheoaks and slim pines,
Adorn the beeches' solid lines.
Lichened boughs, thick and hoary,
Divide to forks of middle storey,
Where orchids peep in purest glory;
Glowing blooms of loveliest tint
Beneath the shadowy canopy glint.

Crystal waters swiftly purl
Below the bracken's tender curl,
Flowing mossy boulders round,
Filing glades with liquid sound.
These ancient forest heritages,
Early forms upon life's stages,
Have endured all Nature's rages.
But after aeons of survival,
Are threatened now by Man's arrival.

Mosses and lichens proliferate,
covering dead and living
timber alike, in damp areas of
Tasmania's beech forests. This
is a portion of Lake Marion
Walk in the Cradle Mountain-
Lake St Clair National Park.

144

It was also late during this Tertiary period that the climate first cooled and aridity began to spread within the continental interior. For the greater part of the following two million years, known geologically as the Quaternary period, almost until the present time, climate was to be significant in producing geographic changes. Periods of wet and dry climate alternated many times. In dry periods desert dunes were formed and built upon, and during wet times lakes formed and enlarged. Wet periods also saw rivers enlarge their channels and flood more extensive areas, depositing alluvium cut from their higher land sources. Temperature also fluctuated widely, dropping sufficiently for ice fields to return. Glaciation was significant, particularly in south-eastern areas such as the Snowy Mountains and in Tasmania. Ice gouged many ranges and plateaus, redistributing soil and rocky debris.

Certainly two, and probably three, of these cold periods or 'ice ages' occurred, locking up so much of the planet's water that sea-levels fell by as much as 130 metres. As a result, coastal valleys were deepened far below present sea-level, Torres and Bass Straits were drained, and the continental shelves became exposed.

The final warning of the climate brought about the last significant changes to Australia's landscapes. Rising seas reflooded the continental shelves and by about 12,000 years ago Bass Strait was refilled to again isolate Tasmania from the mainland. The flooding of Torres Strait followed around 7,000 years ago, separating New Guinea, and by 5,000 years ago the present sea-level had been established and stabilised. Along the coast entrenched valleys were flooded to form inlets and sediments accumulated to build beaches, some with dunes formed by prevailing winds. From that time onward there has been no significant change wrought by purely natural forces, other than the slow and ongoing processes of erosion.

Tall palms (Livistona mariae) *survive in Palm Valley in the Finke Gorge National Park. These trees are living relics of a once widespread species.*

Far Right:
Ghost Gums catch the sunlight as they cling precariously to the deeply fissured and precipitous walls of the Trephina Gorge in central Australia.

It is evident that the bulk of the continent's geographical formation occurred in three broad phases: early formation in Precambrian times as a portion of the ancient Gondwanan supercontinent, separation and primary internal shaping through the Tertiary period, and surface detailing in Quaternary times. These were merged in a gradual but continual process to create the geography of contemporary Australia – a process which spanned aeons.

Equally evidently, many of the major Tertiary events in particular, were regional in nature, giving rise to geological diversity across the continent. In many areas, specially the Central Lowlands and coastal areas which were inundated by the sea, erosion has been severe. In such places it is not uncommon to encounter exposed strata and freestanding or embedded relics of older local rocks. It is the generally eroded local topography, and abundance of such relics that give many vistas their distinctly Australian character.

Edge of rock wall at Kings Canyon Watarrka National Park.

Far Right:
A lone tree sprouts from a rocky knoll in the Kimberley Ranges, but desert grasses dominate these arid regions.

With the exception of Antarctica, Australia is the only 'island continent' not closely abutting another major land mass; thus no description would be complete without mention of the coastline. Including the island of Tasmania, Australia has a seaboard over 35,500 kilometres, varying dramatically in form, and breasting tropical, temperate and semi-polar seas. Seals, whales and penguins frequent this coast, as do vivid tropical fish, colourful sponges and fantastically formed corals.

In some places the shoreline is sheltered and serene, but on much of the coast powerful ocean crashes tumultuously. Tides ebb and flow; in the north-west daily tidal ranges can surpass 50 feet, while on some sheltered south-eastern estuaries tidal effects are quite minimal. Islands dot the coastal waters and the world's largest and most complex coral structure closely parallels a great length of the Pacific seaboard.

In the west, shores are exposed to the colossal forces of waves which have travelled unhindered across vast reaches of the Indian Ocean, and despite the partial protection of some rocky offshore reefs, coastal erosion can be severe. Alluvium forms broad flats, and many headlands are undercut, producing seaward facing cliffs fissured by run-off eroding softer rock formations.

A saltwater crocodile displays the awesome gape of its powerful jaws on a riverbank near Darwin. These highly dangerous creatures are found far upstream and also in the open sea, and have caused many fatalities in Australia's north.

Far Right: Sedges and waterweeds fringe a broad billabong where egrets stalk their prey in a World Heritage area within Kakadu National Park.

South, in the Great Australian Bight, the sea attacks its own former bed. The arid Nullarbor Plain is an ancient sea-floor, chiefly composed of limestone and thinly clad with poor soil. This area was uplifted in the Miocene epoch, roughly 25 million years ago, and even today, many kilometres inland from the present shoreline, the fragile remains of seashells are exposed by winds shifting the sandy soil. Along this coast, the surging Southern Ocean has undercut massive limestone blocks to fashion a particularly rugged series of forbidding, near-vertical cliffs.

In much of the south-east and east of the continent, ancient shorelines are now submerged. The long accumulation of sediments has resulted in a characteristic alternation of rocky headlands and long beaches. Complex inlets have been formed by the sea drowning old river valleys. These provide deepwater sheltered harbours. There are simpler inlets too, cut by relatively young and vigorous rivers, but these are frequently blocked by tidal sandbars. Clean and sometimes rounded sand, deposited by coastal currents, has built up in unbroken stretches easily exceeding 100 kilometres in length. Some of these beaches are pounded by surf, while others line sheltered bays.

Further northward along the eastern seaboard, islands are encountered with increasing frequency in higher latitudes. Many of these islands are steep, thickly wooded and sometimes fringed by coral reefs. These are continental islands; the exposed peaks of a former coastal mountain range. Closer inshore, Fraser Island is an example of an accumulation island. Sand and other alluvium has been deposited by coastal currents, and protected by nearby coastal contours, and populated by wind and water borne vegetation, this has consolidated into a new land formation.

A few other islands to the north – relatively small in both size and number – are true coral islands. These have been formed by the uplifting of solid coral masses and subsequent population by vegetation.

Offshore, parallelling the coastline, stretches the awesome Great Barrier Reef. This astonishing structure is actually a complex of many coral reefs, generally following the crest of the continental slope and extending coastwards across the continental shelf. The outer reefs shelter the inner ones, and the warm, nutrient-rich water gives rise to a multitude of lifeforms. Profuse plankton and reef dwelling fish are a food resource plundered by mammals, birds and reptiles in a complex and self-sustaining ecology. The basis of this phenomenon, the coral polyps, are constantly building upwards and outwards. Their growth ultimately leads to the formation of cays and atolls, each with the potential to become a new islet.

Wildflowers and rock glow warmly in the sunset at the western end of Mount Olga in Uluru National Park, central Australia.

On Australia's northern shores the boundary between land and sea becomes very difficult to define precisely. Here, countless mangroves – about two dozen distinct species – populate extensive mudflats and alluvial reaches. By trapping tidally carried sediments in their intricate root systems, the mangroves are very gradually extending the land seawards. These sediments, slowly enriched by plant detritus, become true soil which is consolidated by invasion of other plant species. Such land reclamation is constant, but exceedingly slow.

The continent's north-western shores also have islands; in some places whole archipelagoes of them. These continental islands are the remnants of the ancient landbridge thought to have once tenuously linked Australia and the south-eastern regions of Asia. Widely-accepted theory is that this landbridge was instrumental in mankind arriving upon the Australian mainland.

The placid waters beneath Nourlangie Rock, Kakadu National Park, in the Northern Territory mirror the fringing Eucalypts and the rugged and richly coloured rock walls.

Humans settled Australia around 30,000 to 40,000 years ago. Accepted theory is that they arrived in the continent across an ancient landbridge that connected the north-west of Australia with the south-eastern regions of Asia. It is likely there were several successive, relatively small scale and gradual migrations by this route; as archaeological evidence points to differing human stocks being involved. Skulls excavated at Lage Mungo and Cow Swamp indicate an apparently concurrent presence of modern human types with a more primitive type, closely resembling Java Man and characterised by flattened and sloping heads with very heavy brow ridges. Following rises in sea-level that submerged the landbridge, both groups would have been left isolated on the Australian mainland. Thus both intermingling of different gene pools, and adaption to the demands of a new environment, have possibly been major factors in the emergence of the Australoid human type. Whatever their origins, Aborigines were present in Australia a very long time before the advent of Europeans to Australian shores.

Generally, the culture of the Aborigines was one of hunters and gatherers. Tribes tended to be nomadic within large but specific areas. Some places were crudely cultivated by certain tribes. This involved burning areas to encourage vegetation regeneration, in an attempt to restock them with natural flora and fauna to ensure future food supplies. Technology was crude; dwellings were slight and temporary, artefacts were few and tended to be both minimal in execution and perishable in nature. Weapons were rudimentary, with the only advances on simple hand-thrown sticks or stones being the boomerang and the woomera, a spinning (and sometimes returning) throwing stick, and a spear throwing aid, respectively. A form of religion based on ancient myths associated with the environment existed, as did a distinctive pictorial art. Overall, population densities were low, with tribes tending to be self-contained and lacking regional cohesion on an intertribal basis.

Grass tussocks and a twisted gum cling to the shallow soil of a rock outcrop in Western Australia's Kimberley Ranges region.

These were significant factors in the subsequent rapid spread of European settlement in Australia. Resistance to European invasion of tribal lands was met with, but by relatively small groups of Aborigines, widely dispersed. This resistance was made ineffectual by the Aborigines' low technological levels and loosely structured culture. This contrasts markedly with the resistance mounted by the tribal peoples of the United States of America, which proved to be a significant hindrance to the extension of European settled areas. In Australia, total tribal subjugation was achieved quickly, though often by employing very inhumane methods.

The dense and unusual growth which gives Palm Valley in the Finke Gorge national park its name.

E xamination of Australia's major statistics immediately reveals a startling contrast – the ratio between area and population. Within a total ara of 7,692,024 square kilometres live over twenty million people (mid-2005) giving Australia a low average population density. More startling is that 80 per cent of the population live on just one per cent of the total land area. Only city-states such as Macao, Hong Kong and Singapore surpass this degree of population concentration into large centres. Indeed, all urban areas combined, occupy only 0.13 per cent of total land area; very little to contain such an overwhelming majority of people.

The population of Australia is most highly concentrated in cities mainly on the eastern, south-eastern and south-western coasts; within areas of fertile soils and equable climate. These cities are surrounded by relatively closely settled coastal zones merging inland into progressively more sparsely populated areas. Within the continent's interior, around 30 per cent of the land is virtually uninhabited.

Nationally then, the pattern of population dispersal is broadly one of a closely settled coastal rim thinning progressively to an uninhabited interior, and

Mossman Gorge Daintree National Park, World Heritage Area.

distinguished by one of the highest degrees of urban concentration in the world. Relative to international standards, population density is very light indeed as Australia is still an historically young and empty continent. It took roughly 200 years from first European settlement for the United States of America to reach a population of 7.2 million in its 1810 census. The Australian population grew to more than double this figure in a similar time span; an impressive achievement, particularly considering Australia's geographical isolation from its major population supply sources.

Despite this growth rate population density remains very light. Densities vary considerably within cities according to distance from commercial precincts or historical centres of initial settlement. A dispersed form of city dwelling or 'urban sprawl' has developed, producing cities of large area but relatively low aggregate population, and density of population also varies according to the architecture of available dwellings; whether detached houses or multi-dwelling apartment blocks.

Fracture planes, scree and weathered surfaces catch the sun's last rays, casting dark shadows upon a rock outcrop in Rainbow Valley in central Australia.

Elsewhere, in rural areas, the norm is determined largely by land use. In the intensive farming areas, from 1 to 4 people per square kilometre is an average density, with small towns occurring at intervals of 30 to 50 kilometres. Less arable areas, used for wheat growing and sheep farming, have population densities which range from 1 person per square kilometre to 1 person per 8 square kilometres, and here small towns are spaced at intervals of 50 to 100 kilometres. Further inland beef cattle are grazed, and human population densities drop very low indeed, and may even fluctuate in accordance to climatic or seasonal variation.

The underlying reasons for this unusual pattern of population distribution are to be found in historical, climatic and geographical factors.

After their inception, the Australian colonies relied on shipping as the major form of transportation, both for coastal trade and for contact with Britain, which was the main source of population and expansionary capital. Subsequent economic developments occurring throughout the 19th century, such as the growth of an export economy based on wool, wheat and gold, together with a heavy and continuing dependence on imports, established the dominance of capital cities with adequate ports.

Bird River in south-western Tasmania burbles gently among ferns and mossy boulders.

Sustained immigration of predominantly urbanised settlers further ensured the growth of the cities, and their continued ascendancy as major population centres.

Most major discoveries of minerals and underground resources such as coal, were made in the nineteenth century and occurred along the continental rim. Thus, the coastal areas offered a reliable climate, the best farming lands, mineral wealth and water; all the elements necessary for the founding of settled areas. Inland there was little to tempt people to establish themselves. Lateral expansion along the coastline was rapid as farm produce and extracted minerals could be readily shipped, and a community social life was possible, but inland penetration offered little but hardship and desolation.

The difficulties of climate and geography which constrained inland expansion remain very considerable. Rocky shallow profile and saline soils are widespread, and despite the availability of some artesian water, the extremely arid conditions and low soil fertility make most inland areas too harsh even for dryland farming. Many areas are sandy or stony deserts. In suitable areas beef cattle are grazed, but this is not a labour intensive pursuit and few significant towns have been established except at major railheads. Some settlement has occurred with mining development at a few commercially valuable mineral deposits, but such settlement tends to be very localised and semi-permanent in nature, existing only while mining remains viable. Even with mining, the economic considerations of being remote from deepwater ports can tend to limit development.

The Finke River, thought to be the oldest river in the world still within its original bed, here reflects shadowed gums, orange banks and the pink sky of sunset.

Prior to European discovery, and subsequent settlement, Australia was fundamentally the same as it is today. Geologically old, geographically stabilised and experiencing a virtually identical climate, it awaited discovery and recognition by the peoples of the world. The remarkably diverse and distinctive flora and fauna were firmly established and ecologically integrated. The continent was sparsely populated with the inhabitants generally concentrated around the fertile permeter areas, and it was free of dangerous predators. Vast quantities of gold and other mineral wealth lay ready to be revealed and exploited. Wonders of the natural sciences lay latent, ready to astound even knowledgeable men. But, despite long-held suspicions of its existence, it remained unknown.

The Malays came to northern Australian shores to fish and trade with coastal tribespeople; but they were simple fisherfolk uninterested in dreams of colonial expansion. The mighty Dutch East India Company envisioned conquest of a land rich is spices, silks, jewels and gold. They had the power, men, experience and risk capital to establish strongholds and exploit the new continent. Dutch ships encountered forbidding coastlines; the bitterly cold bleakness of south-western Tasmania and arid, sandy wastelands along the continent's western shore.

Judging the land inhospitable, and foreseeing no immediate profits, the Dutch East India Company declined to pursue the matter of the Great South Land, or 'New Holland', any further. The opportunity for Dutch colonisation of Australia lapsed.

Almost two centuries later, it fell to James Cook, of humble origins, sailing in a converted collier, to reveal Australia's fertile eastern seaboard. This occurred only as the secondary objective of a scientific voyage in the Pacific Ocean. Subsequent English colonisation was promoted by several considerations, but a major factor was a plethora of felons in Britain, created by harsh social conditions. The first permanent settlement of Europeans was a penal colony. Convicts served their time and free immigrants arrived, slowly building a European population.

Late afternoon light patterns fields along Moralona Drive, here dominated by the ranges walling Wilpena Pound in South Australia.

As the population grew, Australia gradually revealed her richness. The wool and wheat industries flourished and the Australian goldrushes became the world's richest and most remarkable. Exploration revealed vast and fertile areas bordering the inland deserts and agricultural and pastoral activities expanded. By 1901, the various colonies, having achieved autonomy from Britain, federated into a Commonwealth and Australia took her place among the nations of the world. Remote isolation and colonial dependence had matured into regional self-sufficiency and national independence. Continued national growth was assured.

Concurrent with Australia growing, Europe was slowly regressing. Political oppression, industrial exploitation and poverty had become widespread. Discord and the fomenting of rebellion against the established order spread throughout Europe, aggravating further a general social disquiet. The New World, America and Australia, were relatively free of the class stratification and social limitations of Europe and offered the prospect of riches arising from new opportunities in many diverse fields.

Emigration became appealing, especially to practical and enterprising lower and middle class people. Just as in the United States of America, where the Statue of Liberty, inscribed with Emma Lazarus' words:

> "Keep ancient lands, your storied pomp! ...
> Give me your tired, your poor,
> Your huddled masses yearning to breathe free,
> The wretched refuse of your teeming shore ..."

invited migration, so too, Australia lured repressed people with adventurous spirits to sail southwards to a new life.

The view across Lake Pedder to the Mount Franklin Range, in a World Heritage area of Tasmania's Southwest National Park.

The frontiers of the New World had no place for European class constraints and outmoded social repression. People of the lower and middle classes emigrated from Europe in droves. With them came the practical skills necessary to pioneer settlements in remote areas and the seeds of a more vigorous and egalitarian social structure. Pioneering life came to be characterised by an acceptance of only minimal restraint and by cooperation, self-reliance and an indomitable drive towards independence. Herein lay the true and enduring values of the New World, and the Great South Land offered an environment in which they could flourish. Australia's real worth lay not in simple fishing, silks and spices or in dumping convicts; but in fostering human freedoms and forging independence of spirit.

Well within a century of the First Fleet's arrival, Australia was transformed from a dreaded destination of exile and degradation into an inviting land of hope and promise. This remains true today, as evidenced by continuing immigration from both traditional European sources and newer ones. Humanitarian and social values are enshrined in law and custom, opportunities abound for enterprising and industrious individuals, democracy prevails and the nation enjoys political stability. Australia is still seen internationally as 'the lucky country'.

Dead timber protrudes from a coastal sand dune at Discovery Bay Coastal Park in Victoria. Sand ripples and the twisted tree forms attest to the work of predominant winds.

Far Right:
Granite boulders, partially covered by lichen, face the surf at Wilsons Promontory National Park in Victoria.

P art of Australia never actually seen, but very frequently the subject of comment by overseas visitors, is the Australian national character. Everybody, everywhere, is truly unique and individual, but it is also true that most peoples of most nations share particular character traits. Our language is littered with clichés regarding national traits; 'sultry' Spaniards, 'fiery' Irish, 'stolid' Dutch, and 'glum' Swedes are terms commonly encountered and are evidence of a widespread general acceptance that such national traits exist. In this respect Australia is no different to other countries, except perhaps, that no trait is obviously predominant. It is the particular blending of several strong traits which produces the distinctly Australian national character. This in turn creates a type of intellectual and emotional ambience which is experienced by all who cross Australian shores.

A Ghost Gum towers proudly above low scrub in the Western MacDonnell Ranges.

Far Right:
Twilight at The Devils Marbles near Tennant Creek.

In some cases national traits may have obvious causes. The Britons, for example, have earned the appellation of being 'strait-laced'. Clearly, the perspective of the viewer may affect the national trait observed and how it is categorised, and bias is often evident; so too are questions of degree and typicality. Be that as it may, national traits are recognised, but must be combined appropriately to arrive at a point where an entire national character is both recognisable and typical.

In Australia, a multitude of factors have produced a distinctive national character composed of many traits, none of which is clearly pre-eminent. To begin to understand this complex character requires a look at Australia's roots in the not too distant past, and a scanning of the subsequent influences of more contemporary major events.

Australia's first European settlers were the people who arrived in the First Fleet. This initial population, composed predominantly of convicts, was thrust into an unknown and largely inhospitable environment.

The pretty Tooranga River flows among mossy boulders, bordered by forest and ferns, just north of Warragul in the Gippsland region of Victoria.

The convicts came from repressed lower classes, inured almost since birth to a state of hopelessness imposed on them by harsh social conditions, poverty and the rigid British class system. Their punishment was exile, but they were denied by circumstance the opportunity to submerge themselves within some new culture. Instead they adapted the customs they had to fit new circumstances, abandoning some conventions and clinging tenaciously to others. Thus, exile was truly a punishment rather than an escape, and even today a sense of being isolated from the long traditions of Europe and the world's great centres of activity expresses itself in a form of 'cultural cringe' and a reluctance to recognise and nurture outstanding local talents.

Coming from uncharitable circumstances had made the convicts tough. Upon committing an offence and being sentenced to transportation, they endured many months of intolerably subhuman conditions aboard hellish prison hulks and convict transport vessels before reaching New South Wales. Punishment then began in earnest, with the only foreseeable future consisting of regimentation, degradation, appalling conditions and severe physical stress. Few more hopeless situations could be envisaged, yet they remained a lively, if scurrilous lot – as evidenced by the carousing which occurred on the night that the female convicts of the First Fleet were finally landed.

Breaking waves racing beachward glisten and glow in the light of late sunset.

Far Right: Late light shines on the rocks and grasses of Mount Nameless, near the town of Tom Price which is a mining centre in the Hamersley Ranges.

Following months of horrendous confinement, energy was still found for riotous celebration; foolish and misdirected as it may have been. This unlikely buoyancy of spirit, or perhaps mere lust, showed that the first basic stock of later generations possessed a quality essential to coping with the unknown – they were exceptionally durable, indeed natural 'survivors'. This human durability generally produced an attitude of stolid and relentless stoicism, virtually an indispensable quality for a convict who was to outlive his sentence

and attain freedom. The same doggedness of purpose was displayed later by pioneer families and Australian troops at war, and is still often evident among Australians in times of adversity or crisis.

Naturally, other qualities than doggedness were evident in both the initial and subsequent convict consignments. Opportunism is always to the fore among oppressed people as an aid to survival. Optimism was present too, sometimes unrealistically so, as evidenced by several convict escapes and the almost unrealistically-sized landholdings claimed and cleared by some early farmers. Even merriment was occasionally to be discerned, although not spontaneously nor exuberant until circumstances wrought the chance for it to show, for the serious business of survival remained the foremost priority.

Convicts and expired time convicts known as 'ticket of leave men' were joined progressively by free immigrants. Many free immigrants were lower and middle class people dissatisfied by the established order in Europe and evading unjust social conditions and industrial exploitation.

Such people were hardy, skilled, industrious and of sufficiently humble origins to have at least some empathy for the convicts and ticket of leave men.

Together, these groups formed the bulk of a population which was dominated by a small elite group of wealthy and educated people, favoured by the naval and military based official administration. Brutality was commonplace, and European class attitudes were mimicked and sometimes exaggerated by the small elite. A polarisation of society was inevitable and gave rise to widespread, though subdued, attitude of resentment of authority and privilege, which was most commonly given expression as sympathy and support for those seen as unfortunate underdogs. From such beginnings grew an ultimately overwhelming drive towards egalitarianism and equality of opportunity. These traits are all still clearly evident in the contemporary national character.

A rock overhang on Obiri Rock within the World Heritage area of the Kakadu National Park.

Far Right:
Egrets are silhouetted above the burnished surface of Yellow Water Billabong as the sun rises over the Kakadu National Park.

Most early settlers were agricultural or pastoral pioneers, pushing the frontiers of settled land ever further from the niceties of civilisation. These hardy folk were pre-eminently practical and faced considerable hardship and peril in remote localities. Western notions of family privacy and insularity were deep rooted and rigorously preserved, yet a degree of 'tribalisation' occurred as a result of remoteness. This was because of the need for interfamily cooperation to achieve enormous and urgent tasks such as shearing, ploughing and harvesting. It was also a survival need. In times of peril such as bushfire or flood, only cooperative effort offered any chance of avoiding total annihilation. Similarly, neighbours were often the only source of succour when accident or illness struck. This led to a large degree of bonding between the mostly self-reliant families within districts. From this cooperation came a concern for community interests, strong local loyalty and an acceptance of others on a basis of equality; all character traits still common in Australia today. Rural cooperation also nurtured mateship, that deep adult bonding based on mutual respect and reliance over a long period. Such relationships transcend social ones and are characteristic of the deep and enduring friendships still frequently formed and fostered by many modern Australians.

White trunked River Gums with blue-green foliage, backed by cliffs of pinkish hue, reflect in the still waters of a pool within Ormiston Gorge in the Northern Territory.

Far Right: The sculptural forms of water-worn boulders are accentuated by moss and lichen in this rainforest stream near Babinda in Queensland.

Hence a basis was laid capable of accommodating the next major advance of the Australian people; the unprecedented and explosive population growth which resulted from the discovery of gold. The goldfields of New South Wales and Victoria especially, appeared almost spontaneously and grew with alarming rapidity. Cities and farms were almost deserted, and immigrants poured into the diggings. With so many people, mostly newcomers, congregated in small areas, it was impossible for the authorities to cope adequately. Crowded conditions narrowed the options to chaos or cooperation. The cooperation established by rural communities was the model followed. It was clearly the only workable choice if the goldfields were to be exploited successfully and profitably with full participation by individuals and small groups. Consequently, an informal but effective cohesion was established by the people themselves, rather than by formal authoritarian direction and imposition. This community cohesion worked well; the Australian goldfields were remarkable both for their richness and general lack of serious unruliness.

This was a triumph for the common people in overcoming the privileged elite they had come to resent. Cosmopolitanism was embraced (with the notable exception of non-acceptance of the Chinese by some diggers), egalitarian

principles were reinforced by the sheer bulk of new immigrants and both individual and communal cooperation became evermore essential both in mining activity and everyday life. The authorities imposed directions and levies upon this burgeoning mining population; but as their actions did not reflect either the common good or common will of the people, resentment flared. This culminated in the outbreak of civil rebellion at the Eureka Stockade in Ballarat. As a result of this incident, universal manhood suffrage was achieved, and power passed from the elite into the hands of the common

The Cascades, a charming formation in the Blue Mountains National Park, close to Katoomba in New South Wales.

Far Right:
Cart wheels in Barossa Valley Vineyard.

people. Individual rights were now to be asserted more freely and people generally became more independent in action. This independence of the individual is now a national character trait.

As the alluvial gold petered out, mining became the province of well capitalised companies rather than individuals. Acts of legislation were passed concerning land tenure, which enabled selections of land to be made from squatters' traditional holdings. This was intended to assist in accommodating the swollen population in traditional farming pursuits. Overall, this policy failed to achieve its objective, but the privileged class, large landholding squatters, were reduced in regional economic importance and legislative influence. However, small scale farming was not economically viable in the longer term, and the depopulation of rural areas and a major growth in cities resulted. The 'average Australian' was no longer a bushman, but an urban dweller engaged increasingly in commercial and industrial pursuits rather than the various aspects of primary production.

Throughout the nineteenth century and well into the twentieth, two dominant gender stereotypes existed. Women were expected to be genteel, motherly where appropriate, as refined as their circumstances permitted, and domestically oriented with a devotion to homelife. Men were generally the sole family breadwinners. They were expected to be gallant, hardy, fearless, financially sound and competitive in work pursuits; and to a degree, authoritarian in family matters. Any marked degree of departure from the appropriate stereotype, for either gender, was likely to attract quite severe censure and social disapproval. Although these stereotypes are currently modified extensively, and community attitudes have softened considerably, such dated stereotypes exist today, particularly among the older generation.

Thorny Devil on red sand dune in Central Australia.

Far Right:
Treeferns have established dominance in this section of the Tara Valley, near Yarram in Victoria. These are extremely slow-growing plants and the length of their moss-covered trunks indicates their great age.

The catalyst in bringing about stereotype change and adaption was the advent of war. Both the major world conflicts played a cumulative role in freeing men and women from overly restrictive gender roles.

With manpower reduced by military requirements, and additional productive capacity needed to generate war matériel, women were freed of the constraints of home life and entered the spheres of commerce and industry which were formerly the preserves of men. Having gained entry, they remained for the duration of the war, and then continued throughout peacetime too. Similarly, they accompanied men to war, creating a stronghold for themselves initially in the professional nursing arms of the naval, military and airborne services. Here too, their presence was welcomed and was destined to continue. For men, war wrought elemental changes also. The new technical sophistication of warfare tended to suppress individuality and promote a regimented conformity. Individual acts of selfless heroism still occurred, but to be fearless was superhuman and frequently suicidal. Egoism was modified by the dictates of survival, and humility learnt in the face of stupendous military power.

The changes wrought were irreversible. In peacetime, particularly in family life, men were no longer sole breadwinners and economic despots, and so could afford to shed their authoritarian images and show their humanist values. Fathers were now able to become approachable, concerned and involved 'Dads'. Women were no longer homebound creatures full of refinement but short of practical intellect, and found greater freedom personally and financially. Femininity bloomed more freely and more fully. Such broad modifications to gender stereotypes were not sudden and dramatic, but resulted from a slow process occurring through both World Wars and the intervening Depression era.

Kangaroos gaze curiously towards the camera from amid wildflowers in northern Australia.

Far Right:
Drowned trees are silhouetted by the rising sun which reflects in the misty waters of the Murray River.

BARRIER REEF

Beneath the creaming breakers rolling for the Queensland shore,
Sprawl vivid coral jungles hosting living things galore.
Amid this twisting complex, stretching near a thousand miles,
Are labyrinths of reefs and rocks, and chains of sun-drenched isles.
Countless coral multitudes build upwards to the light,
Creating jewelled atolls, oft with fringing sands of white,
Then topped by waving palm trees, to present a wondrous sight.

Here swoops the mighty manta ray to reap the plankton swarms,
While bright and branching nereids stretch forth fantastic forms.
The silvery slim torpedoes of fierce barracuda loom
Around the outer channels through the ocean's ink-blue gloom.
On sunlit surface waters old enormous turtles glide;
In coral crusted crevices strange crabs and crayfish hide.
Antennae probing cautiously for food swirled by the tide.

In the shallow tidal races bright and garish shellfish crawl;
On wavelet lapped white beaches stranded jellyfishes sprawl,
For life is in a frenzied state, each day sees death and birth,
In a vast marine habitat – the greatest one on earth.
Coral grows relentlessly; for the sunlight reefs are aimed,
Sands are trapped, fish die – their nutrients are soon reclaimed;
In the cycles of this process, new land from life is gained.

A shaft of sunlight and the delicate glistening veil of Liffey Falls brighten this sombre Tasmanian gully.

Far Right:
A boat pulls to the jetty at Green Island, on the Great Barrier Reef east of Cairns in northern Queensland. This island is famed for its underwater coral observatory.

Where then, have these deliberations of successive changes brought us? We may now propose a description of a 'typical Australian', in the hope that the national character will be revealed. Such a person is an urban dweller but likely has ancestors of a rural background. They are the product of a closed family in which they participated in an intimate and humanist family relationship. As a member of a democratic society this person is personally independent, egalitarian in outlook and probably charitable and sympathetic to the less fortunate 'underdog' elements of their community. He or she is usually cooperative and can be quite dogged in chosen pursuits, and is likely a participant in an enduring mateship.

All of this is broadly true and much of it is statistically verifiable. But it is not yet complete, for change is a constant process. Postwar, the pace of change has quickened. Social phenomena of a global nature such as oral contraception, the feminist movement, American-dominated television, Asian immigration and broadscale environmental pollution are all of sufficient magnitude to produce social changes which may affect the national character. What these factors produce is a matter for coming generations of Australians.

Rugged scenery in the Amphitheatre, seen from Initiation Rock in the Finke Gorge National Park.

Certainly the specific character traits identified as major elements of the 'typical Australian' person are of great importance, indeed are a central factor, in determining national character; but considerably more is required. Quite evidently, great variation from this norm exists within a significant proportion of the populace when they are considered on an individual basis. Age, gender, ethnic background and socio-economic factors may vary even with 'typical' Australian types. It is also obvious that the national character itself is subject to continual change and development as time progresses. A broader view is required, one which allows for individual variation as well as ongoing changes.

Two broad and important factors are the society which hosts and affects the national character, and the culture which is its outwardly visible expression. Society may be considered as the composite structure formed by the aggregation of both individuals and groups; and culture as the activities engaged in by individuals and groups within that framework.

Australian society is an amalgam of many different national groups in which multiculturalism has always found an uncommonly reasonable level of acceptance, and it is now actively promoted as official policy. During the goldrush era and before Australia's Federation in 1901, most immigrants came from the various nations of Europe, but by the end of the century immigration from other areas of the world began to outstrip the European intake.

The rolling hills of Gippsland's Strzelecki Ranges are fertile farmlands. This view from near Seaview in Victoria, is from these hills and across the Latrobe Valley in the distant Baw Baw Range.

Far Right:
Extensive weathering of these sedimentary rocks has produced flanged forms at Keep River National Park in the Northern Territory. Wildflowers bloom profusely whenever moisture permits it.

A large population of immigrants have intermarried and become integrated into Australian society, enriching it with a diversity of cultural heritages. Consequently, a cosmopolitan factor has been introduced to such varied elements of Australian life as cuisine, architecture and sport; yet without displacing other earlier forms.

Society is also composed of many groups other than ethnically or nationally based ones. Many quite highly structured groups exist. These include the Church in all its forms, academic communities such as in universities, trade onions and professional associations, political parties, sporting and recreational organisations and many others; each with their own accepted, and often codified, modes of behaviour. More generalised and unstructured groups also exist, often only identifiable by a certain commonality of attitudes or behaviour. These include such diverse and amorphous groupings as 'greenies', 'ockers', 'wowsers', 'boozers' and 'punters' and may reflect either specific interests, socio-economic or even geographically influenced factors. So society is a multi-layered construct.

Ferns, rotted timber and mosses attest to the damp conditions found around cascades; these are at Lady Barron Falls in Tasmania's Mount Field National Park.

Far Right:
Hummock grass and pale-barked Ghost Gums dot the red soil of a Kimberley Ranges hillside in Australia's north-west.

Culture is a term often equated with the higher human endeavours in art, theatre, music, dance and literature or with the history or folkart of the indigenous people. While Australia is quite rich in these areas, especially for a young nation, and has achieved enviable international acclaim, this view of what constitutes culture is too restrictive and narrow.

Such pursuits as ballet or sculpture are simply the 'tip of the iceberg' and may be termed 'high culture'. Conversely, communally frowned upon activity such as painting graffiti may be recognised as a form of 'low culture'. Between these two extremes the great bulk of Australian culture lies in the province of everyday activities, both creative and non-creative, and may be termed 'popular culture'. Popular culture is far wider, more varied and more pervasive than either high or low culture. It is embedded in the innumerable ways people relate to each other, in the language chosen to express ideas and opinions, in the humour of jokes and cartoons, in community attitudes and in popular music. It is how people choose to relax, be it watching the football or races, playing at the park or inviting friends to a barbecue in the backyard.

Popular culture is diverse and dynamic; the people shape it and it leaves its mark upon them all. Attitudes fostered on sporting arenas – and sport has a big influence in Australia – are translated and carried over into business and family life. Even climate and architecture play indirect roles; clearly the open shopfronts and bustling street life of Asia would be inappropriate in Hobart or Melbourne, so local equivalents develop. Popular culture even includes taxation and trade unionism, as they contribute to shaping attitudes of cooperation, communal ownership and the Australian expectations of employers and government.

These three factors determine the national ambience: typical individuals, the Australian social structure and Australia's popular culture. Combined en masse they create a national ambience which is truly unique, distinctively Australian and instantly apparent to participants and observers alike. Like the land from which it sprang, it is often both warm and rugged.

Misty morning on Wallaga Lake.

However, national character is far more than a phenomenon which can only be viewed en masse, for it is an ethos which exists within individuals as well as within the Australian populace as an entirety. Therefore, to consider the whole without considering the individual elements must lead to a falsely incomplete conclusion. Broadly typical groups engaged in 'popular' cultural activities undoubtedly create an Australian ambience in which the national character resides and can find expression – but the *essence* of that ambience, the national character itself, is most clearly evident on an individual level. It shows itself in the underlying attitudes of most Australian people; in their humour, expectations of themselves and of others, and in the sources of their pride or embarrassment.

The national character is a matter of heritage. It is transmitted from generation to generation by the influence the foregoing generation exerts on the current generation. It is broad and general in its nature and results from the influence of all adults upon all children; thus persisting despite the variation of specific opinions and attitudes which always exist among individuals or even family groups. As a form of heritage, it has its genesis in the history of Australia's

early development; in the way that traditional customs and beliefs brought from older established countries have been modified to fit the conditions of Australian life.

This heritage of national character is encountered by children as a process in which adults, by example and by imposition, gradually shape each child's attitudes as to what is 'right' or acceptable. Generally, what is 'right' in one family, group or school is usually 'right' in others, so a cumulative effect is produced which reinforces concepts of the 'rightness' of many attitudes. This reinforcement is so strong that most children 'instinctively' learn what is 'right' or 'wrong', in terms of attitude as well as moral judgement, well before their teen years and carry the same concepts through into adult life. Often it is not apparent until later years that there are alternative ways of reacting to circumstances and that none of them is necessarily 'right'. Only then does the selection or adoption of appropriate attitudes become a predominantly personal or arbitrary matter.

A small jetty is silhouetted and duplicated as a reflection on the burnished surface of Wallis Lake near Forster on the coast of New South Wales.

Because of this heritage, some generally accepted Australian behaviour patterns, such as the machismo of many men which is often expressed as a disregard for physical comfort or as a refusal to show sentiment, may actually seem offensively harsh and unfeeling to other people of different nationalities. Such attitudes of emotional stoicism and proud hardihood had their roots in the tough independence of pioneers constantly facing adversity: hardened settlers accustomed to scorning newcomers they considered "too soft for this country".

Clearly, the harsh land and severe social conditions of early settlement altered the behaviour patterns of Australia's forefathers in a manner that has survived through subsequent generations and continues to affect people today. Similarly, other national traits may be traced back in time; Australian attitudes of resentment towards authority and a widespread acceptance of egalitarianism are a legacy of the convict era and the great economic depressions of the 1890s and 1930s. These have survived and been modified to become assimilated into urban modes of behaviour despite their outmoded and rural origins.

A small stream winds its way through the lush rainforest near Babinda in Queensland.

Far Right:
The upright form of a solitary tree emphasises the flatness of stubble covered plains in the wheat growing Wimmera region of Victoria.

Other greater and more recent events have wrought even stronger changes to the national character, notably the major global wars. In the first global conflict Australia, as a young and newly independent nation, involved herself fully and acquitted herself creditably. This experience stripped away any feeling of inferiority which had accompanied colonial status and established a strong sense of national identity. Today, this is expressed as proud nationalism and a strongly competitive spirit.

The second major war had a tremendous influence on Australia's national character. Women gained greater independence and became an integral part of the workforce, gaining for themselves increasingly important roles in social, civic and political spheres. Australia was opened up to foreign influence when hundreds of thousands of American troops were stationed on her soil. Marriages resulted and permanent cultural ties became established, reinforced by a military alliance which saw America, not Britain, become Australia's major partner and protector. This reversal of British influence and increasing American influence notably through news media, politics and trade, is an ongoing process still both controversial and active. It is having, and will continue to have, a profound effect on Australia's national character.

The attack on Darwin and fareast to Australia's northern shores brought a realisation to Australians that their physical presence was in Asia and Oceania, despite their predominantly European origins and outlook. Immigration policies had long been actively pursued, but as Asian intakes began to outstrip European ones, the conviction that Australia's future was interwoven with Asia's was substantially reinforced.

Mist shrouds the Gordon River in a steeply cut gorge in Tasmania's Wild River National Park.

Hence, contemporary Australia is European in origin and outlook, Asian by regional context and politically aligned increasingly with Washington rather than London. Her immediate national future lies in confronting the problem of uniting or reconciling these disparate influences – or being torn asunder by them.

These then, are the influences affecting and shaping contemporary Australians. They are industrious, unpretentious and comradely folk in general, possessed of a strong individuality. Specific personalities are as diverse and colourful as those found elsewhere in the world, but a deeper element exists, a character shaped by the foregoing historical and geopolitical factors. Beyond the individuality of Australians lies an independent, dynamic, fair minded and forward looking national character.

Barham River Otway Ranges near Apollo Bay.

ULURU NATIONAL PARK

From desert sands and endless plains abruptly up they rear;
Aged and weathered monoliths, dome-topped and rising sheer,
Sharp silhouettes unblurred by growth and standing starkly clear.
Mount Olga raises rounded heights; distinctive shaping given
By curving forms, fissured clefts – rocks from each other riven.
While vast Uluru, Ayers Rock, with huge breathtaking size,
Towers ever upwards red and stern, to challenge azure skies.

Man's petty peccadilloes are naught within its presence,
Lasting awesome strength are in its elemental essence;
Being in our modern world Man's egoism it lessens.
Perhaps the value of this stone lies mute upon its face,
Uluru lasts, an ancient symbol of a mystic race,
While Man's bright sciences, which vaunt of gaining glory high,
Are but a phase in Time's long stream, to pass completely by.

Ayers Rock (Uluru), the world's
largest monolith, juts 349
metres above the plains of Uluru
National Park. Here, framed
by trees, the colour is softened
by the wash of moonlight.

Australia's surface, despite its aridity and the urbanised concentration of its population, is rich and varied in landforms, vegetation, fauna and human cultural heritage. Beneath the surface, the continent has also proven to be exceptionally rich. Sub-surface riches, in the form of organic fuels and mineral ores, form the base of Australia's diversified industrial capacity as well as a substantial export trade.

Extensive deposits of both black and brown coal, natural gas and oil have been discovered and developed. Large reserves of uranium exist and some of these have been developed for the export market. All major metals are to be found in abundance and most minor metals are relatively plentiful.

Snow Gums pierce the mantle of snow covering Mount Feathertop and the Southern Alps, viewed from Mount Hotham in Victoria.

Australia is self-sufficient in most minerals of economic importance, and has such surplus in some that large-scale export is practical and economically viable. Major minerals with proven reserves adequate for projected domestic demand and excess for export include bauxite, black coal, clays, copper, diamonds, gold, iron ore, lead, manganese, natural gas, nickel, salt, silver, tin, uranium and zinc. In addition, there are commercially viable resources producing antimony, bismuth, tantalum, titanium, tungsten, vanadium and zirconium.

Much of Australia's mineral wealth results from the continent's vast and varied geological age. Most of the western and central areas of the continent consist of basement rocks of Precambrian age, and major mineral deposits such as at Broken Hill, Mount Isa, Olympic Dam, Kalgoorlie and within the Pilbara and Alligator Rivers regions occur in these very ancient rock zones. Younger Palaeozoic rocks, mostly of geosynclinal origin, form a discontinuous belt several hundred kilometres in breadth, extending from northern Queensland to Tasmania.

Folded rock strata show on a weathered bluff at Mount Buffalo in Victoria.

Right:
A white Heron wings gracefully across the Yellow Water Billabong in Kakadu National Park.

Far Right:
Large 'magnetic' termite mounds rise from the plains near Litchfield Conservation Park. Their north to south alignment ensures maximum exposure to the sun's warmth.

Within this zone major base metal deposits occur at Alura, Cobar, Woodlawn and Rosebery, as well as most of the nation's black coal deposits. However, the black coal of Queensland's Moreton district, north-east of New South Wales and South Australia were formed within a broad zone of Mesozoic platform sediments extending southwards from the Gulf of Carpentaria. Younger still, are the deposits formed in Tertiary times. These include Victoria's brown coal, bauxite at Weipa, Gove and the Darling Range and also the nickeliferous laterites at Greenvale in Queensland.

The first indication of Australia's mineral wealth came in September 1797, when Lieutenant John Shortland found coal on the banks of the Hunter River. During the early 2000s, New South Wales and Queensland provided over 95 per cent of Australian black coal production, most of which was won underground. Total measured and indicated black coal reserves at that time were 45,500 million tonnes, with inferred deposits greater than 76,000 billion tonnes. Most of this is bituminous coal and more than half of the black coal won is exported.

Curiously eroded rocks in the Lost City formation in Litchfield Conservation Park exercise the imagination. This one vaguely resembles a giant human.

Far Right:
Lake Argyle is Australia's largest reservoir and was created by the damming of the Ord river in 1972.

In 2003 Australia was the world's third largest producer of brown coal. Brown coal is found in Victoria, where it is used primarily for electricity generation. The measured and indicated reserves for brown coal are 37.6 billion tonnes.

By contrast with coal, Australia's oil resources are small relative to the rates of extraction and demand, and oil must be imported. Most proven oil reserves lie offshore in Bass Strait, with relatively small resources operating in Western Australia, South Australia and southern Queensland. Recent onshore and offshore exploration and development in many areas – especially in Australia's north-west region – hold considerable promise of ameliorating the nation's oil shortage situation. The last half of the 1980s saw an accelerated oil exploration activity and significantly successful results being achieved. Production is now about 75 per cent of domestic demand.

Another potential source of energy is uranium for use in atomic reactors. This is a controversial issue and currently Australia does not use atomic power domestically. However, large uranium reserves exist and have been mined intermittently. First uranium mining was in 1954, and continued to the early 1960s when it was discontinued. Major uranium discoveries occurred in the 1970s in the Northern Territory, Western Australia and South Australia, and in response to a revival of world markets and a relaxation of government mining and export controls, production for uranium export commenced again. Australia has the world's largest resource of recoverable uranium and is the second largest producer after Canada.

Bright coral grows in a tidal rockpool on Queensland's Whitsunday Reef.

Far Right:
Near Jamestown in South Australia, a rainbow forms as sunlight is refracted by a passing rain shower.

Iron ore is abundant in Australia. For a variety of conservation and strategic reasons the Australian government prohibited the export of iron ore between 1938 and 1960. By the end of this period total iron ore production was little more than 4 million tonnes, all of which was consumed domestically. The lifting of the export ban in 1960 was shortly followed by the announcement of huge discoveries of iron ore in the Pilbara region. By 1977, total output passed 100 million tonnes, of which over 80 per cent was exported, making Australia the third largest iron ore producer in the world. Production has fluctuated for a number of reasons and domestic consumption has increased, but in 2002 Australia was the world's largest exporter and third largest producer of iron ore, behind China and Brazil.

Tree lined waterhole in the
Ormiston Gorge National Park.

Commercial mining of bauxite began in Australia in 1963. From bauxite, refining produces alumina (aluminium oxide). Alumina may then be electrolytically smelted to produce the metal aluminium. Only a small proportion of Australian bauxite is processed into aluminium for domestic use. However, in 2003 Australia was the world's largest producer of bauxite and the largest producer and exporter of alumina. Recent investments in refining and smelting operations are aimed at increasing the export of the finished product, aluminium.

Copper was first discovered in Australia by Captain Bagot and Francis Dutton in 1842 when they located rich deposits of copper carbonate ore at Kapunda in South Australia. Since that time more than 2000 copper deposits have been worked or investigated, but most were quickly exhausted or proved not to be commercially viable. Major copper mines are at Mount Isa in Queensland and Olympic Dam in South Australia. Smaller projects are found in New South Wales, Queensland, Western Australia and Tasmania. Although copper is refined for domestic use and a little is exported, most exports are in the form of concentrates to supply overseas refineries. Australia's annual production is about 869,000 tonnes, and as a producer ranks fourth in the world behind Chile, USA and Indonesia.

Lead and zinc usually occur together, often with silver and even copper. For many years, Australia has been one of the world's leading producers of lead and zinc, and the largest exporter of lead. The two major producing areas are Mount Isa and Cannington in Queensland. Several other deposits have been the subject of intense exploration and assessment.

Sunlight casts deep shadows and glows on grasses and high cirrus clouds along Western Australia's Gunbarrel Highway.

Nickel ore and concentrates have been gaining prominence among Australia's mineral exports. Annual production was 188,000 tonnes in 2003, ranking Australia as the world's second largest producer. Nickel is only mined in Western Australia.

Mineral sands produce a number of rarer ores. Sand mining is carried on and Australia is the world's largest producer and exporter of rutile, ilmenite and zircon. These ores have specialised applications in high technology metallurgy and ceramics.

When one thinks of minerals and mining, it is often the 'glamorous' wealth of gold and diamonds which immediately springs to mind. Even in these exotic minerals Australia has proven tremendously rich. Since the 1850s gold has been mined in Australia and it has been acknowledged as one of the richest sources of this precious metal anywhere on the globe. In 2003, Australia produced 284 tonnes of gold, ranking Australia equal second with the United States for production.

A ray of sunlight glows upon the rich colours of the rock walls at the head of Kings Canyon in central Australia.

Diamonds have a less active and colourful history than gold. Their first recorded discovery was in 1851, the same year that the first goldrushes began in earnest, but these were small stones of little commercial value. Diamonds were mined on a very small scale in New South Wales between 1872 and 1922 but no really significant finds were made. Airly Mountain near Lithgow yielded some stones in the 1930s and spasmodic mining continued until the 1980s but large deposits did not eventuate. In 1978 a major find occurred at Argyle in the Kimberley region of Western Australia. The Ashton Joint Venture commenced mining in 1983 concentrating first on the alluvial and scree deposits capping the AKI kimberlite pipe. In 1986 mining commenced within this pipe and won 29,210,764 carats of diamonds. This production from the one mine easily exceeded the entire annual diamond production of any other country. Australia is indeed 'the lucky country'!

This book set out to produce a portrait of a unique and fascinating land. The fine photographs contained herein achieve that aim admirably and artistically. The text has attempted to sketch some aspects of the nation that the camera could not capture. The only way in which the subject of the portrait can begin to be known is by personally experiencing the uniqueness and fascination of Australia and her people.

Late afternoon sunlight casts long shadows across the lush wetlands of Kakadu National Park, viewed from Obiri Rock.

Top:
Water colours indicate depths in a portion of the Whitsunday Reef, showing corals have grown upwards a considerable distance from the sea-floor.

Bottom:
Stormy sunset sky over Norman Island, Wilsons Promontory National Park.

Far Right:
Tree limbs bow and rocks are capped as snow settles over the Nature Trail in Victoria's Mount Buffalo National Park.

HIGH COUNTRY'S WINTER

Silent cold white blanket
Descends from leaden sky,
Bowing twig and branchlet,
Concealing ground from eye.
Silent; breeding silence,
Dulling each bushland sound,
A chilly soundless ambience,
Affecting all; profound.

Greenness cedes to whiteness,
Gloomy or blinding bright,
Alpine lands surrender
To winter's icy night.
Icicles suspended
In crystal stalactites,
Mark where streamlets have now ended,
Pure waters frozen tight.

No birdcalls sweet resound
In echoes from the peaks,
No wallabies abound
By burbling mountain creek.
Until spring thaws the range —
Brings vivid blooming change;
Renewing sap's full upward flow
And bushland's softly vibrant glow.

GLOSSARY

Aborigines – a race of tribal people who were the earliest inhabitants of Australia.

Acacia – any tree or shrub of the *Acacia genus*, usually known as "wattles" in Australia.

Allocasuarina – a genus comprising both trees and shrubs commonly known as "sheoaks" in Australia. *A. torulosa* is a species found in Queensland and New South Wales which is a small to medium conical tree with rough corky bark. Its pendulous branchlets are subject to reddening.

Alluvium – sand, mud, gravel, etc. deposited by the action of flowing water.

Ambience – the environment or surrounding atmosphere of a place especially pertaining to its mood, quality or character.

Antarctic Beech – a tree of the *Nothofagus* genus: survivors of the ancient Gondwanan flora.

Australoid – an ethnic group of peoples inhabiting Australia and also parts of Asia and the Pacific islands, who share certain physical characteristics.

Banksia – any tree of shrub of the *Banksia* genus named for botanist Sir Joseph Banks, characterised by leathery leaves and cylindrical heads of flowers, commonly known in Australia as "bottlebrush".

Banyan – any tree, usually of the *Ficus* genus or fig group, which drops roots from its branches to the ground enabling it to spread over a wide area.

Baobab – a large, exceedingly thick-trunked tree of the genus *Adansonia* native in both Africa and Australia.

Barchan – a sand dune, often crescent shaped with downwind pointing horns, asymmetric in profile, with the gentler slope on the convex or windward side and the steeper slope on the concave or leeward side. Such dunes are commonly mobile, progressing as windborne sand from the convex side tumbles down the leeward slope.

Belah – the common name of *Casuarina cristata*, a conical tree which grows to about 12 metres tall and has a wide distribution in drier areas.

Billabong – a waterhole in a creek or the anabranch of a river which is isolated, may dry completely in drought periods, and is replenished only by rainfall or during flood times.

Biotica – windborne and waterborne organic matter such as seeds, pollen, ova and even minute creatures which are carried from one region to another.

Boomerang – a piece of hardwood, usually bent or curved and used as a missile by Aborigines. One form when correctly thrown, curves about in flight to return to the thrower.

Boronia – any of a number of shrubs of the genus *Boronia* characterised by aromatic foliage and highly perfumed flowers.

Bottle tree – a tree of the special *Brachychiton* which grows to 20 metres and is characterised by a swollen bottle-like trunk.

Bossiaea – any shrub of the 40 or 50 species comprising the genus *Bossiaea* which are characterised by small pea-flowers, often in yellows and brown. Commonly it is referred to as "eggs and bacon".

Brachycome – a genus of small perennial plants with daisy-like flowers.

Brigalow – a wattle, *Acacia harophylla*, which is often dominant and extends over large areas of Queensland and northern New South Wales.

Burrs – a plant bearing seeds encased within a rough and prickly cover. Low growing and drought-resistant burrs of many species are common in certain desert areas.

Burthen – an outmoded nautical term relating to the maximum burdened weight of a ship; similar to displacement tonnage.

Cassia – any of about 28 species of the *Cassia* genus of shrubs which are characterised by heads of many small flowers.

Chorizema – a genus of about 18 species, all but one being endemic to Western Australia. They are shrubs and twiners which produced masses of orange and/or red pea-flower blooms.

Convict transportation – a penal system whereby convicted felons were sentenced to exile. In its day it was seen as a humane alternative to capital punishment, but in practice it was usually an excessively cruel form of slavery.

Cordylines – a genus of plants characterised by long, tapering leaves radiating from slender, palm-like trunks.

Correa – a small endemic genus of about 10 species characterised by winter flowering of tubular blooms.

Crowea – a genus of woody shrubs which bears open star-shaped blooms and flowers during winter.

Cyprus Pine – any of the 16 species of the genus *Callitris*, one of Australia's relatively few conifers.

Deciduous – the habit of shedding leaves at a particular time, usually annually at the onset of winter.

Depression – a meteorological term for an area of low atmospheric pressure. In the southern hemisphere depressions are accompanied by clockwise winds.

Desert Oak – any tree of the *Acacia decaiseana* species, which has a termite resistant timber and occurs in central and north-western Australia.

Detritus – disintegrated material, especially finely broken down debris.

Dingo – the Australian wild dog, *Canis familiaris dingo*, first introduced by the Aborigines, but now feral.

Dolerite – an igneous rock, usually coarse-grained and resembling basalt.

Dune – a sand hill or sand ridge formed by the wind, usually in deserts or on beaches.

Egalitarian – believing in and asserting the equality of all people.

Epacris – any of the low shrubs of the *Epacris* genus, which includes some heaths, characterised by open or tubular blooms and small, often spiky, leaves.

Epiphytic – plants which grow upon host plants but do not obtain food, water or minerals from that host. Many epiphytes can extract water directly from humid air.

Epoch – the main division of a geological period, representing the time required for making a geological series.

Eremophila – any bush of the 180 species of the *Eremophila* genus, commonly called "emu bushes" or "poverty bushes". They are characterised by tubular flowers and a great variety of foliage forms.

Erosion – the processes by which surfaces are worn away by the action of water, wind, glaciers, waves, etc.

Evapo-transpiration – loss of precipitation by a combination of direct climatic evaporation and the transpiration of moisture by plant life.

Fauna – a collective term for all animal life of a region or continent.

Ferntree – any fern which progressively regenerates from the centre, slowly building a fibrous trunk.

Flora – a collective term for all plant life in a region or continent.

Genus – (*pl* genera) the usual major biological or botanical subdivision of a family or subfamily, usually consisting of multiple species, essentially very similar to one another and closely related.

Geosyncline – a portion of the earth's crust subsiding for a long time, prevalently linear and usually containing great thicknesses of sedimentary and volcanic rocks, often re-elevated at a later time.

Glacier – an extended mass of ice moving very slowly.

Golden Wattle – the *Acacia pycnantha*, Australia's national floral emblem which has masses of small, globular blooms of bright yellow.

Grasstree – any grass, usually long and spiky, which progressively regenerates from the centre, slowly building a fibrous trunk.

Grevillea – any of the 250 species of the *Grevillea* genus, most of which are endemic to Australia and are characterised by various brush-like forms of blooms.

Hardenbergia – a genus of climbing twiners which produces purple pea-flowers in abundance.

Helichrysum – this is a large genus of the Asteracea family which is distributed globally, but around 100 species of *Helichrysum* are endemic to Australia. They have daisy-like blooms.

Helipterum – like *Helichrysum* this is a genus of the Asteracea family and has daisy-like blooms.

Herbaceous – plants with non-woody, non-persistent stems, usually flowering annually before dying away to regenerate the following year.

Hovea – a small genus of 12 species of small woody shrubs which are characterised by purple pea-flowers.

Igneous – rock formed from magma which has cooled and solidified.

Jarrah – a large tree, *Eucalyptus marginata*, of Western Australia's open forests which is valued for its durable dark red timber.

Karri – another tree valued for its durable timber, *Eucalyptus diversicolor* grows rapidly and is confined to Western Australia.

Laterite – a reddish, iron-rich soil formed in tropical regions by the decomposition of underlying rock and characterised by a porous concretionary crust.

Leptospermum – is a widely distributed genus of about 40 species, commonly known as "teatree".

Littoral – pertaining to the shore of a lake, sea or ocean but especially the zone between low and high tide levels.

Marsupial – mammals which have a pouch which contains the mammary glands and is a receptacle for the developing offspring. Most, but not all, marsupials are native to Australia, and include kangaroos, wombats, possums and other animals.

Melaleuca – a large genus of 140 species of shrubs and trees, many of which occur in boggy situations and are commonly called "paperbarks".

Metamorphic – a type of rock which has undergone a structural change usually as the result of heat and/or pressure.

Midstorey – that section of a forest which grows midway between ground level and the upper canopy of leaves.

Millennium – a period of a thousand years (*pl.* millennia).

Monolith – a single piece or block of stone of considerable size.

Monsoon – the rainy season of northern Australia occurring from December to February brought by the seasonal wind which blows from the south-east in winter and the north-west in summer.

Monotremes – the lowest order of mammals, found only in Australia, and consisting of the platypus and the echidna, the only mammals to lay eggs externally.

Mountain Ash – a very large tree, *Eucalyptus regnans*, often dominant in the open forests of eastern Australia.

Mulga – a small tree or large shrub, *Acacia aneura*, which is often multi-stemmed and rises to widespread dominance in arid areas.

Olearia – a large genus of around 100 species, *Olearia* occurs in Australia, New Guinea and New Zealand but about 80 species are endemic to Australia. They are small to large woody shrubs with daisy-like blooms in white, blue, pink or mauve.

Oxylobrium – an endemic Australian genus of about 30 species of woody plants ranging from prostrate to medium-sized trees. They bear pea-flower blooms in yellows and reds and many have interesting foliage.

Period – the main division of a geological era, represented in the earth's crust by systems of rocks formed during it, and divided into epochs.

Plankton – a collective term for minute animal and plant organisms drifting through the seas.

Polyp – an individual sedentary animal, fixed at the base of a columnar body and provided with an open mouth and tentacles. Coral polyps are colonial and excrete a hard calcerous substance which forms coral reefs.

Precipitation – naturally condensed water occurring as rain, dew, mist, snow, etc.

Promontory – a projection of land or rock into the sea, surrounded on three sides by water but connected to the main land mass.

Proteaceae – a large plant family which includes the banksias and waratahs.

Saltpan – a basin or low-lying area flooded by saline water periodically or the remains of an evaporated salt lake crusted with salt crystals.

Scree – a mass of rocky detritus, usually in a steep slope at the base of a precipice or monolith.

Sill – a tabular body of intrusive igneous rock usually between layers of sedimentary rock and/or volcanic tuff.

Stalactite – a deposit, usually of calcium carbonate, formed by the dripping of percolating calcerous water, hanging from the roof of a limestone cave or suchlike site.

Stalagmite – an inverted stalactite growing upwards from the floor of a cave.

Stoicism – conduct following the Stoic philosophy that men should be free from passion, unmoved by joy or grief, and submit without complaint to unavoidable necessity; generally, the repression of emotion and an indifference to pleasure or pain.

Strata – layers of rock, usually sedimentary rock, formed one atop another in parallel layers (*sin.* stratum).

Styphelia – a genus of about 12 species of small woody shrubs with long tubular flowers of green, pink or red.

Syzygium – a genus with several species of trees. *Syzygium luehmannii* grows to 30 metres, has a buttressed trunk and the young growth is red or bright pink. It grows in Queensland and New South Wales.

Taxa – a general term relating to categories; taxonomy is the science of classification.

Tectonic – pertaining to the structure of the earth's crust especially major crustal plates, their movements and disruptions such as earthquakes, folding and faulting.

Telopea – a genus of the Proteaceae family with only 4 species; the waratahs.

Understory – the lower level of growth in forests or plant groupings which is protected by the canopy of upper leaves.

Volcano – a vent in the earth's crust through which molten lava, ash, steam and fumes are expelled to form a conical heap about a central crater.

Volcanic intrusion – the intrusion of molten rock (lava) under pressure beneath or between other rock formations causing distortion of that rock formation's prior shape.

Volcanic plug – the exposed vent of an extinct volcano, usually bared by erosion of softer rock from about the solidified lava.

PHOTOGRAPHIC DATA

2 AYERS ROCK, N.T.
Mamiya RZ67 250mm lens ½ sec. at f32 on Fuji 50

9 CAPE CONRAN, VIC.
Makina 67W 55mm lens $1/_{125}$ sec. at f8 on Fuji 100

11 CAPE BRIDGEWATER, VIC.
Mamiya RB67 65mm lens $1/_{125}$ sec. at f5.6 on Fuji 50

13 GREAT AUSTRALIAN BIGHT, S.A.
Mamiya RZ67 110mm lens $1/_{125}$ sec. at f11 on Fuji 50

15 WADDY POINT, QLD.
Pentax 6x7 105mm lens $1/_{60}$ sec. at f11 on Fuji 50

17 THOUIN BAY, TAS.
Leica R4 90mm lens $1/_{125}$ sec. at f4 on Kodachrome 25

18 PINE VALLEY, TAS.
Mamiya RB67 65mm lens ½ sec. at f22 on Ektachrome 64

21 ST COLUMBA FALLS, TAS.
Pentax 6x7 45mm lens $1/_{30}$ sec. at f11 on Fuji 50

23 MAINGON BAY, TAS.
Mamiya RZ67 50mm lens ¼ sec. at f16 on Fuji 50

25 BEN BOYD NP, N.S.W.
Linhof Technorama 6x12cm 65mm lens ¼ sec. at f22 on Fuji 50

29 NEAR WYNDHAM, W.A.
Bronica ETRS 75mm lens $1/_{60}$ sec. at f11 on Fuji 50

31 PINNACLES, QLD.
Makina 67W 55mm lens $1/_{60}$ sec. at f16 on Fuji 100

33 SUGARLOAF BAY, N.S.W.
Mamiya RZ67 250mm lens $1/_{30}$ sec. at f5.6 on Fuji 50

34 CASCADES, NEAR PEMBERTON, W.A.
Mamiya RZ67 50mm lens ½ sec. at f22 on Fuji 50

35 CAPE KERAUDREN, W.A.
Mamiya RZ67 50mm lens $1/_{15}$ sec. at f22 on Fuji 50

36 WONNANGATTA-MOROKA, VIC.
Leica R4 28mm lens $1/_{30}$ sec. at f8 on Fuji 50

37 GANTHEAUME POINT, W.A.
Mamiya RZ67 50mm lens ¼ sec. at f16 on Fuji 50

39 FEDERATION PEAK, TAS.
Bronica ETRS 40mm lens $1/_{60}$ sec. at f4 on Kodachrome 25

41 WADDY POINT, QLD.
Linhof Technorama 6x12cm 135mm lens $1/_{30}$ sec. at f22 on Fuji 100

43 BAOBAB, KIMBERLEY RANGES, W.A.
Mamiya RZ67 50mm lens $1/_{15}$ sec. at f16 on Fuji 50

45 FLINDERS RANGES, S.A.
Walton-Rogers 6 x 12 cm 65mm lens $1/_{15}$ sec. at f22 on Ektachrome 64

47 GEIKE GORGE, W.A.
Mamiya RZ67 50mm lens $1/_{125}$ sec. at f11 on Fuji 50

48 WARATAH, N.S.W.
Leica R4 60mm lens $1/_8$ sec. at f16 on Kodachrome 25

49 JAMISON VALLEY, N.S.W.
Makina 67W 55m lens $1/_{30}$ sec. at f22 on Fuji 100

50 CAMBRIDGE GULF, W.A.
Nikon F3 300mm lens $1/_{15}$ sec. at f5.6 on Kodachrome 25

51 THE THREE SISTERS, N.S.W.
Mamiya RZ67 180mm lens $1/_{15}$ sec. at f16 on Fuji 50

53 GLASSHOUSE MOUNTAINS, QLD.
Mamiya RZ67 50mm lens $1/_{60}$ sec. at f16 on Fuji 50

55 PINE VALLEY, TAS.
Mamiya RB67 65mm lens ½ sec. at f16 on Ektachrome 64

57 ST. HELENS POINT, TAS.
Walton-Rogers 6x12cm 65mm lens ½ sec. at f22 on Ektachrome 64

58 CAPE NELSON, VIC.
Mamiya RB67 65mm lens $1/_{15}$ sec. at f22 on Fuji 50

61 CARNARVON GORGE, QLD.
Makina 67W 55mm lens ½ sec. at f22 on Fuji 100

63 CEPHISSUS FALLS, TAS.
Toyo 45A 90mm lens 1 sec. at f22 on Ektachrome 64

65 MOUNT FEATHERTOP, VIC.
Mamiya RZ67 180mm lens ¼ sec. at f16 on Fuji 50

66 EVERLASTING DAISIES, VIC.
Mamiya RZ67 110mm lens $1/_{30}$ sec. at f16 on Fuji 50

67 LAKE BULLA, VIC.
Mamiya RZ67 50mm lens $1/_{15}$ sec. at f22 on Fuji 50

69 MURRAY RIVER, NEAR LOXTON, S.A.
Bronica ETRS 40mm $1/_{60}$ sec. at f8 on Fuji 50

70 STURT'S DESERT PEA, S.A.
Mamiya RZ67 180mm lens $1/_{15}$ sec. at f16 on Fuji 50

73 ELDER RANGE, S.A.
Linhof Technorama 6x12cm 135mm lens with Polarizer ½ sec. at f22 on Fuji 50

75 THE LABYRINTH, TAS.
Mamiya RB67 65mm lens $1/_{30}$ sec. at f16 on Ektachrome 64

76 FLINDERS RANGES, S.A.
Mamiya RB67 65mm lens, $1/_{60}$ sec. at f16 on Fuji 50

79 MORALANA DRIVE, S.A.
Mamiya RZ67 50mm lens ¼ sec. at f16 on Fuji 50

81 LAKE WINDERMERE, TAS.
Mamiya RB67 180mm lens $1/_{15}$ sec. at f16 on Ektachrome 64

83 FINKE GORGE, N.T.
Mamiya RZ67 50mm lens $1/_{30}$ sec. at f22 on Fuji 50

84 PELION EAST, TAS.
Mamiya RB67 65mm lens $1/_{60}$ sec. at f16 on Ektachrome 64

85 NAMBUNG, W.A.
Mamiya RZ67 50mm lens $1/_{15}$ sec. at f22 on Ektachrome 64

87 HAMERSLEY GORGE, W.A.
Mamiya RZ67 50mm lens $1/_{30}$ sec. at f16 on Fuji 50

89 MOUNT OLGA, N.S.
Walton-Rogers 6x12cm 65mm lens ½ sec. at f32 on Ektachrome 64

90 ROSELLAS, QLD.
Nikon F3 200mm lens $1/_{125}$ sec. at f5.6 on Fuji 50

91 DAINTREE RIVER, QLD.
Mamiya RZ67 50mm lens $1/_{60}$ sec. at f11 on Fuji 50

93 PEMBERTON, W.A.
Mamiya RZ67 180mm lens ¼ sec. at f22 on Fuji 50

95 EUCLA, W.A.
Linhof Technorama 6x12cm 65mm lens ¼ sec at f22 on Fuji 50

101 COOPER CREEK, S.A.
Mamiya RZ67 50mm lens $1/_{30}$ sec. at f22 on Fuji 50

105 CHAMBERS PILLAR, N.T.
Linhof Technorama 6x12cm 135mm lens $1/_8$ sec. at f16 on Fuji 50

106 BOY MARTIN POINT, N.S.W.
Makina 67W 55mm lens $1/_{125}$ sec. at f16 on Fuji 100

107 SILLERS LOOKOUT, ARKAROOLA, S.A.
Bronica ETRS 40mm lens $1/_{125}$ sec. at f16 on Fuji 100

109 CHARLOTTE PASS, N.S.W.
Makina 67W 55mm lens $1/_8$ sec. at f16 on Fuji 50

111 NEAR ESPERANCE, W.A.
Mamiya RZ67 180mm lens with Polarizer $1/_{30}$ sec. at f11 on Fuji 50

113 RUSSELL FALLS, TAS.
Makina 67W 55mm lens $1/_{60}$ sec. at f8 on Fuji 100

115 NOOSA, QLD.
Pentax 6x7 45mm lens $1/_8$ sec. at f16 on Fuji 50

117 FINKE RIVER, N.T.
Mamiya RZ67 250mm lens $1/_{15}$ sec. f16 on Ektachrome 64

120 DEVIL'S MARBLES, N.T.
Makina 67W 55mm lens $1/_{60}$ sec. at f16 on Fuji 100

125 PORT DOUGLAS, QLD.
Mamiya RZ67 50mm lens $1/_{60}$ sec. at f11 on Fuji 50

126 MCKENZIE FALLS, VIC.
Mamiya RB67 65mm lens $1/_8$ sec. at f16 on Ektachrome 64

127 SNOWY RIVER, N.S.W
Toyo 45A 90mm lens $1/_{30}$ sec. at f11 on Ektachrome 64

129 KATHERINE GORGE, N.T.
Linhof Technorama 6x12cm 65mm lens ¼ sec. at f16 on Fuji 100

131 JEWEL CAVE, W.A.
Mamiya RZ67 50mm lens 20 sec. at f11 on Fuji 100

134 KING SOLOMONS CAVE, TAS.
Leica R4 24mm lens 25 sec. at f8 on Kodachrome 25

135 REMARKABLE ROCKS, S.A.
Mamiya RZ67 50mm lens $1/_{15}$ sec. at f22 on Fuji 50

139 NEAR ADELAIDE RIVER, N.T.
Mamiya RZ67 50mm lens $1/_{30}$ sec. at f11 on Fuji 50

142 LAKE PEDDER, TAS.
Pentax 6x7 300mm lens $1/_{30}$ sec. at f11 on Fuji 50

143 HALLSTON, VIC.
Mamiya 645 super 80mm lens $1/_{125}$ sec. at f8 on Fuji 50

145 LAKE MARION WALK, TAS.
Walton-Rogers 6x12cm 65mm lens
8 sec. at f32 on Ektachrome 64

146 PALM VALLEY, N.T.
Mamiya RZ67 50mm lens $1/_{60}$ sec.
at f11 on Ektachrome 64

147 TREPHINA GORGE, N.T.
Mamiya RZ67 250mm lens $1/_{15}$
sec. at f16 on Fuji 50

149 KIMBERLEY RANGES, W.A.
Mamiya RZ67 50mm lens $1/_{60}$
sec. at f16 on Fuji 50

150 CROCODILE NEAR DARWIN, N.T.
Contax 167MT 200mm lens $1/_{125}$
sec. at f8 on Kodachrome 64

151 KAKADU NP, N.T.
Mamiya RZ67 180mm lens $1/_{30}$
sec. at f8 on Fuji 50

153 MOUNT OLGA, N.T.
Mamiya RZ67 50mm lens $1/_8$ sec. at f22 on Fuji 50

155 NOURLANGIE ROCK, N.T.
Mamiya RZ67 180mm lens $1/_{30}$
sec. at f16 on Fuji 50

157 KIMBERLEY RANGES, W.A.
Pentax 6x7 45mm lens $1/_{30}$ sec.
at f22 on Ektachrome 64

159 PALM VALLEY, N.T.
Mamiya RZ67 127mm lens $1/_{30}$ sec.
at f16 on Ektachrome 64

163 RAINBOW VALLEY, N.T.
Linhof Technorama 6x12cm 65mm
lens ½ sec. at f16 on Fuji 50

165 BIRD RIVER, TAS.
Linhof Technorama 6x12cm 65mm
lens 8 sec. at f32 on Fuji 50

167 FINKE RIVER, N.T.
Mamiya RZ67 90mm lens ¼ sec.
at f16 on Ektachrome 64

169 MORALANA DRIVE, S.A.
Mamiya 645 super 150mm lens
1/30 sec. at f11 on Fuji 50

171 MOUNT WARNING, N.S.W.
Nikon F3 300mm lens ¼ sec. at
f5.6 on Kodachrome 25

172 DISCOVERY BAY, VIC.
Mamiya RB67 65mm lens $1/_{60}$ sec. at f16 on Fuji 50

173 WILSONS PROMONTORY, VIC.
Leica R4 28mm lens $1/_{30}$ sec. at
f8 on Kodachrome 25

174 GHOST GUM, MACDONNELL RANGES,
N.T.
Mamiya RZ67 65mm lens $1/_{60}$ sec.
at f16 on Ektachrome 64

177 TOORONGA RIVER, VIC.
Linhof Technorama 6x12cm 65mm
lens $1/_{30}$ sec. at f16 on Fuji 100

178 BREAKING WAVE AT ST. HELENS POINT,
TAS.
Pentax 6x7 300mm lens $1/_{125}$ sec. at f4 on Fuji 50

179 NEAR TOM PRICE, W.A.
Pentax 6x7 45mm lens $1/_8$ sec. at f22 on Fuji 50

180 OBIRI ROCK, N.T.
Mamiya RZ67 50mm lens $1/_{30}$
sec. at f16 on Fuji 50

181 YELLOW WATER BILLABONG, N.T.
Bronica ETRS 40mm lens $1/_{60}$
sec. at f5.6 on Fuji 100

182 ORMISTON GORGE, N.T.
Mamiya RB67 127mm lens $1/_8$ sec.
at f16 on Ektachrome 64

183 BABINDA, QLD.
Mamiya RZ67 180mm lens ½
sec. at f22 on Fuji 50

184 CASCADES NEAR KATOOMBA, N.S.W.
Makina 67W 55mm lens ½ sec. at f22 on Fuji 100

187 TARRA VALLEY, VIC.
Leica R4 180mm lens ½ sec. at
f16 on Kodachrome 25

188 RED KANGAROOS, S.A.
Nikon F3 300mm lens $1/_{125}$ sec. at f4.5 on Fuji 50

189 MURRAY RIVER, N.S.W.
Leica R4 90mm lens $1/_{60}$ sec. at
f5.6 on Kodachrome 25

190 LIFFEY FALLS, TAS.
Toto 45A 125mm lens ½ sec. at
f22 on Polarchrome 100

191 GREEN ISLAND, QLD.
Mamiya RZ67 50mm lens $1/_{15}$
sec. at f11 on Fuji 50

193 AMPITHEATRE, N.T.
Walton-Rogers 6x12cm 65mm lens
¼ sec. at f16 on Ektachrome 64

194 NEAR SEAVIEW, VIC.
Mamiya 645 super 80mm lens
1/30 sec. at f11 on Fuji 50

195 KEEP RIVER, N.T.
Bronica ETRS 40mm lens $1/_{30}$
sec. at f22 on Fuji 50

196 LADY BARRON FALLS, TAS.
Toyo 45A 75mm lens 1 sec. at
f32 on Polarchrome 100

197 KIMBERLEY RANGES, W.A.
Mamiya RZ67 180mm lens $1/_8$
sec. at f22 on Fuji 50

201 WALLIS LAKE, N.S.W.
Makina 67W 55mm lens $1/_{125}$
sec. at f5.6 on Fuji 100

202 BABINDA, QLD.
Mamiya 50mm lens ½ sec. at f22 on Fuji 50

203 WIMMERA, NEAR WARRACKNABEAL, VIC.
Pentax 6x7 105mm lens $1/_{15}$ sec. at f16 on Fuji 50

205 GORDON RIVER, TAS.
Leica R4 90mm lens $1/_{60}$ sec. at
f2 on Kodachrome 25

209 AYERS ROCK, N.T.
Walton-Rogers 6x12cm 65mm lens
1 sec. at f22 on Ektachrome 64

211 MOUNT HOTHAM, VIC.
Linhof Technorama 6x12cm 65mm
lens $1/_{60}$ sec. at f16 on Fuji 100

212 MOUNT BUFFALO, VIC.
Leica R4 28mm lens $1/_{30}$ sec. at
f5.6 on Kodachrome 25

213 WHITE HERON, YELLOW WATER
BILLABONG, N.T.
Nikon F3 300mm lens $1/_{500}$ sec. at f5.6 on Fuji 100

213 NEAR LITCHFIELD CONSERVATION
PARK, N.T.
Bronica ETRS 40mm lens $1/_{60}$
sec. at f16 on Fuji 50

214 LOST CITY, N.T.
Bronica ETRS 40mm lens $1/_{60}$
sec. at f16 on Fuji 50

215 LAKE ARGYLE, W.A.
Bronica ETRS 40mm lens $1/_{60}$
sec. at f16 on Fuji 50

216 WHITSUNDAY REEF, QLD.
Nikon F3 55mm Macro lens $1/_{60}$
sec. at f11 on Fuji 50

217 NEAR JAMESTOWN, S.A.
Mamiya RZ67 250mm lens $1/_8$
sec. at f16 on Fuji 50

221 GUNBARREL HIGHWAY, W.A.
Pentax 6x7 45mm lens ¼ sec. at
f16 on Ektachrome 64

223 KINGS CANYON, N.T.
Walton-Rogers 6x12cm 65mm lens
¼ sec. at f16 on Ektachrome 64

225 KAKADU NP, N.T.
Walton-Rogers 6x12cm 65mm lens
½ sec. at f16 on Ektachrome 64

226 WILSONS PROMONTORY, VIC.
Leica R4 180mm lens $1/_8$ sec. at
f5.6 on Kodachrome 25

227 MOUNT BUFFALO, VIC.
Mamiya RZ67 50mm lens $1/_{60}$ sec. at f8 on Fuji 50